Listening to the Animals

BEST FRIENDS

A GUIDEPOSTS BOOK

ACKNOWLEDGMENTS

Every attempt has been made to credit the sources of copyrighted material used in this book. If any such acknowledgment has been inadvertently omitted or miscredited, receipt of such information would be appreciated.

All material that originally appeared in *Guideposts* magazine or *Daily Guideposts* is reprinted with permission. Copyright © 1992, 1993, 1995, 1996, 1997, 1998, 1999.

"The Funniest-Looking Cat" is from *Cats* by Beth Brown. Copyright 1970 Beth Brown.

"Smuggling a Gift From the Sky" is from *A Search for the Perfect Dog* by Gary Shiebler. © 1997 Gary Shiebler. Published by Broadway Books.

"The Cat Who Came Home" is from *Sasha's Tail* by Jacqueline Damian. © 1995 Jacqueline Damian. Published by W. W. Norton & Company.

"Make Yourself Comfortable, Rufus" is from *The Rufus Chronicle* by C. W. Gusewelle. Copyright 1996 C. W. Gusewelle. Published by The Ballantine Publishing Group.

"The Fastest Dog on Earth" is from *My Dog Skip* by Willie Morris. © 1995 Willie Morris. Published by Random House, Inc.

"Yes, Dogs Can Speak!" is from *Stillmeadow Sampler* by Gladys Taber. Copyright 1959 Gladys Taber.

"A Conspiracy of Cats" is from *A Cat Is Watching* by Roger Caras. © 1990 Roger Caras. Published by Simon & Schuster, Inc.

"Bandit, the Fashion Hound," by Craig Williams, is from *Unforgettable Mutts* by Karen Derrico. © 1999 Karen Derrico. Published by New Sage Press.

"Doggy Baggage," by Eleanor Garrell Berger, is from *Our Best Friends* by Michael Capuzzo and Teresa Banik Capuzzo. © 1998 Michael Capuzzo and Teresa Banik Capuzzo. Published by Bantam Books.

"The Hippo and the Antelope" is from *Dogs Never Lie About Love* by Jeffrey Moussaieff Masson. © 1997 Jeffrey Masson. Published by Crown Publishers, Inc.

"The Noble Dog," by George Graham Vest, is from a nineteenth-century inscription on a monument outside a Missouri courthouse.

"The Undercover Cat" is from *The Best Cat Ever* by Cleveland Amory. © 1993 Cleveland Amory. Published by Little, Brown and Company.

"The Case of the Lonely Swan" is from *It's a Jungle Out There* by Gary Richmond. © 1996 Harvest House Publishers.

"Second Puppyhood" is from *Poultry in the Pulpit* by Alexander Cameron. © 1988 Alexander Cameron. Published by St. Martin's Press.

"Good Night, Honey" is from *Stillmeadow Sampler* by Gladys Taber. © 1959 Gladys Taber.

"Mrs. Donovan" is from *James Herriot's Dog Stories.* © 1986 James Herriot. Published by St. Martin's Press.

(continued on page 209)

Designed by SMS Typography
Illustrations by Gary Halsey
Jacket designed by Dennis Arnold
Printed in the United States of America

Contents

CARING WHEN IT COUNTS

GENTLE TEACHERS

MAKING A DIFFERENCE

LOVE THAT DOESN'T END

Introduction

Getting to know an animal is the beginning of a very special relationship. At the start, we don't speak the same language, we may not even walk on the same number of feet, and while some of us will fly or swim in deep waters, the rest of us will stay on dry ground. Yet something brings us together. Perhaps by accident, perhaps by design, we meet, and our lives are changed forever. We become friends. As we learn to understand each other's ways, language doesn't matter. Being together does. We give each other God's greatest gift: love. No strings attached.

Over the years, the editors at Guideposts have been touched by the response of readers to our many stories about animal and human friendships. Now we feel it is time to bring you a feast of true accounts of people and animals who love each other and make each other's lives richer. This is a book about the devotion that only best friends share.

We begin with DISCOVERING EACH OTHER, stories that describe the many different ways people and animals meet, such as Beth Brown looking for something fancy at a cat show and coming away with a homely kitten who claimed her heart. Or Gary and Linda Shiebler trying to cross the border with an irresistible stray—with a beard!—who had begun following them in Tijuana, Mexico.

The meeting of the animal and the person is only the beginning of the discovery. After that comes a time of learning about each other and how they enrich each other's lives. C. W. Gusewelle was determined that his bird dog, Rufus, was going to live outdoors, until Rufus changed his mind and not only came inside but took over the easy chair. Gladys Taber discovered that a dog's bark can tell you what is going on around you—if you know how to listen.

The stories in CARING WHEN IT COUNTS tell us how much it means to have an animal—or a person—beside you when you need a friend. Cleveland Amory's cat, Polar Bear, snuggles under the covers of his hospital bed. And Alexander Cameron makes us chuckle even as we admire the devotion of the Murgatroyds, who insist on staying close to their dog while he undergoes eye surgery.

GENTLE TEACHERS is an inspiring collection of stories about animals who show us how to meet life's challenges. Keesha, a beloved German Shepherd who was stricken with cancer, enables her owner to fight the same disease with faith and dignity. A disabled raccoon befriends a young woman who needs to learn that there is always hope.

In MAKING A DIFFERENCE we meet animals and people who change each other's lives for the better. Larry Chamberlain takes in a stray dog whose trust in him gives him the strength to stop drinking. Kristin von Kreisler finds the courage to endure an earthquake when her pets stay close by her side. Bonnie Coleman loves her horse so much that she gives her to a girl who can take better care of her.

Those of us who have loved animals can rejoice in these relationships. But at the same time we are haunted by the knowledge that we probably will outlive them. In LOVE THAT DOESN'T END, we learn how to deal with that reality. We discover that even when we have to part, the love remains. Bert Clompus is reminded of his friendship with a nameless cat who leaves her kittens in his care. Mary Jane Stretch will always remember and cherish a deer she raised and released back into the wild. And a family will always be grateful that a brave, blind little chicken graced their lives for almost two years.

As for who is the best friend, the animal or the person, these true stories make it clear that probably it is both. Each has a special love and respect for the other. But anyone who has been privileged to share a friendship with an animal will tell you that it is the animal who teaches us how to be a best friend in return. It's almost as if God were sending us a blessing by way of these wondrous creatures.

PHYLLIS HOBE

BEST FRIENDS

DISCOVERING EACH OTHER

"The whole of the life of another being fitting into a part of your own. . . ."

HENRY AND MARY ELLEN KORMAN

Many of life's most interesting stories tell us how best friends meet. Quite often they aren't even looking for each other, and may not realize that they need a best friend. Then, perhaps unexpectedly, their paths cross, and once they meet, something happens. Lives come together and love begins. Nothing is quite the same again, yet everything is better because the friends have each other.

Some people call it coincidence. Some call it a blessing. Best friends call it a gift from God.

"We'll Take Her!"

ROBERTA MESSNER

Several years ago, our beloved dog disappeared. Family and friends organized a search to find her, but with no success. Each day, I'd anticipate the affectionate thump, thump of her tail lulling me to sleep in my bed. How could I ever make it without her?

Then, one day, the TV newscaster announced the arrival of some beagle puppies at the local pound. Late one Monday afternoon, my husband Mark and I drove over to check them out. "The beagles went fast," the animal caretaker said, "but you might want to consider one of our other dogs."

Discouraged, I plodded from cage to cage, studying the signs posted on their doors. "Landlord says, 'No pets.'" "Owner too old to care for dog." Above the yelps and barks of at least fifty hopeful adoptees, Mark hollered, "Have a look at this one!"

Cleo was four years old and resembled a giant, double-stuffed Oreo cookie. She didn't come close to being a beagle or a puppy. "Older dogs make such wonderful pets," the caretaker said. "This one's already housebroken." As if on cue, Cleo cocked her head in the most endearing pose and extended a fuzzy white paw.

Searching for a clue to Cleo's past, I read the giant hand-written black letters aloud. "'PTS Tuesday.' What does that mean?"

The caretaker hung her head, and I strained to hear her speak. "Put to sleep Tuesday."

"We'll take her! We'll take her!" Mark and I pronounced as we scooped a snuggling Cleo into our arms.

"Let's name her Monday," I suggested.

It's been seven years now, and while we didn't actually change Cleo's name, she'll always symbolize Monday to us. In our time of loss, God rescued us both. And, oh, the joys of adopting a loving, older dog! What seemed to be a "PTS Tuesday" was really a brand-new Monday.

The Funniest-Looking Cat

BETH BROWN

---

*E*ver since I can remember, there has always been a cat in my life.

Of course, my world was not always a big bouquet of red roses. There were times when I lived in an attic on bread and beans along with the nebulous dream of becoming a famous author.

Yet, good days or bad, bright times or dark, fortune or misfortune, a cat always purred on the hearth, very often when no fire burned in the fireplace.

When I was poor, my cat companion was a stray I picked up on the street. When I was rich, my carrying case contained an elegant showpiece with yards of trailing pedigree. I aired that pedigree with proper pride in my jaunts on Riverside Drive, fully aware of the wide-eyed stares at the sight of a cat, walked just like a dog, at the end of a leash. I met the barrage of questions by explaining that I needed the benefit of daily exercise in the open air even more than my four-legged escort.

In time, my neighbors came to know the status of my bank account by the walking barometer beside me. Mixed breed meant minus. Pedigreed meant plus. Of course, when fortune outstripped misfortune, I collected several cats which I added to my growing menagerie of dogs, birds and turtles. Somehow, no matter what the season, it was always raining cats and dogs in my life.

Among my star boarders were cats on loan, cats being boarded sans board for my friends and cats adopted in—to be adopted out. This policy usually ended up by my acquiring the boarders I merely had offered to board.

My cats were collected in devious other ways.

The Cat Show, for instance, would come to town. Here was the cue for me to immediately take my departure.

Instead, I remained behind to face the barrage of telephone calls from well-meaning friends and relatives.

How about another cat?

It was no use reminding them that I had all the cats I could handle. I had more than I could afford to feed and time to air and patience to housebreak.

Why lose a great opportunity? Why not at least take a look at the felines on display?

Of course, I succumbed to their blandishments. I dropped in on the Show.

As a newspaper reporter, I had covered many an opening night in the theatre as well as the various events at Madison Square Garden and the Coliseum.

But as far as I was concerned, here before my spellbound gaze was the most stupendous, gargantuan, supercolossal attraction of all time. In a giant wave of smell, I caught the scent of feline flesh and fur. In a great swell of sound, I heard the sweet music of meowing and purring. My heart pounded. My blood danced. My head was high on cloud nine.

I bought a catalog.

I began walking.

No. I floated through space hung with elegant feline portraits.

Here were hundreds of cats of assorted breeds collected from every corner of the earth and displayed like the most precious jewels, which they were to their exhibitors.

The cats came in various colors and patterns.

There were black cats.

There were white cats.

There were striped cats.

There were patchworked cats.

There were calico cats.

There were tortoiseshell cats.

There were even cats of Russian blue to match my new Easter suit.

The breeds were even more diversified.

There were Siamese cats.

There were Burmese, Abyssinian, Persian and Manx cats.

There were Coon cats.

There were cats as plain as bread and butter and moderately priced, and cats as fancy as a six-layer wedding cake and suitably labeled: *Priceless.*

Surely, out of so many, I told myself, before the day was over I might consider adding just one little pedigreed member to my mongrel collection at home. I had always longed to own a white Persian. In my mind's eye, I saw just the right cat displaying its breathless beauty on my hearth. The Persian exhibit, an attendant informed me, was somewhere or other in the west wing of the arena.

Spectators mulled all around me. Owners and breeders and eager exhibitors paraded past in a surging sea of faces as I hurried down the aisle, my sails all set for a Persian.

Then, don't ask me how it happened.

Suddenly, I found myself standing in front of a cage. Inside sat an ugly, cross-eyed, bowlegged, short-haired contestant. Her eyes were small. Her tail was fat. Her fur was flat. She was a far cry from the breathless elegance of a Persian.

But there was something in the face of that cat which fascinated me. I drew closer. So did she. She rose from her corner and came toward me. Her look, warm, wise and knowing, was my undoing. Forgotten was the elegant white Persian. Forgotten were my reservations.

In some miraculous manner, the little Siamese made the proverbial leap known only to cats. I found her in my arms. In quick succession, she was mine. We were driving back together. We came into the house, and in less time than it takes to spell Supercalifragilisticexpialidocious, she was right at home—where Siamese Empress had every right to be!

from CATS

Smuggling a Gift From the Sky

GARY SHIEBLER

I have always been a big-dog kind of guy. My experience with little dogs has been very limited. My mom had a rather yappy little dachshund named Juliet when I was a boy, but my memories of her are sketchy. She had this unfortunate habit of waiting in the middle of the road until my mom got home from work. One day she just didn't get out of the way fast enough.

"No one even stopped," Mom said.

My next-door neighbor had a very old pug that waddled around the house with buggy, drippy eyes and a bark that can be described only as a heavy smoker's hack in miniature. I am still convinced she was part June bug.

I grew up with an assortment of retrievers, collies, and shepherds. Dogs you could tackle on the front lawn after a long day at school or hug with all your might without fear of hurting them. I had never imagined a small dog being part of our family.

Until a little dog with a beard came into our lives.

In the fall of 1993, I decided to answer a rather ambiguous ad in a San Diego newspaper for a teaching position in Tijuana, Mexico. It was for an after-school program that taught English as a Second Language to students from surrounding schools. Although I had a bachelor's degree and some teaching experience, I didn't have all the course requirements needed to receive a California teaching credential. Unless I was willing to go back to college, I could not teach in the public school system. So I applied at the Queen Elizabeth Institute in Tijuana.

Since our arrival in California, I had abandoned my acting and modeling career and worked in jobs ranging from selling advertising to telemarketing personalized refrigerator magnets. I was at my wit's end, unemployed, angry, and convinced that no one ever got work from the want ads. "You gotta know somebody, you gotta have connections," I wailed.

I got the job.

I would like to say that I got hired because of my sterling résumé and sparkling interview. But I learned later from one of the other instructors that the primary reason I had been hired was that I had curly blond hair and blue eyes.

"It is very important to the headmaster at the institute that the American teachers *look* American," he told me.

As it turned out, they were also looking for someone to teach arts and crafts. My wife had taught art in a number of summer programs.

"Don't worry," I told her while she was blow-drying her long blond hair one night after taking a shower. "You're a shoo-in."

So for the next three years, we would cross the U.S./ Mexican border twice a day, four days a week.

Going into Mexico was rarely a problem. Coming back into the United States was often quite an adventure.

A very dirty and hungry dog had wrapped her paws around my wife's leg as she stood waiting in front of a shoemaker's kiosk a couple doors down from the school.

"I've never been hugged by a dog before," Linda said. "She wouldn't let go. And isn't she cute? Look at those sweet eyes! And the beard! Look at that beard!"

She did indeed have a beard. A very long and scraggly one. It was the first thing you noticed about her. I gave Linda that "last thing we need is another dog" look as she cradled the little street terrier in the school courtyard. After all, we already had two dogs and three cats.

We were soon surrounded by students. The little bearded one charmed them all. Linda told her story about how she had found her.

"She is a gift from the sky, a gift from the sky!" cried one girl.

We named her Cielo—sky.

Our plan was to hide Cielo under Linda's heavy winter coat on the floor by her feet. In our two years crossing the border, our car had rarely been searched. Most of the time we were asked a couple questions regarding our purpose for being in Mexico and whether we had anything to declare. I remembered a sign at the border checkpoint that said it was illegal to bring any *produce* or *livestock* into the States and since a fox terrier didn't fit into any livestock category I knew, we decided that we weren't breaking any laws by trying to bring her home.

We felt confident. I would remain cool, casual, and matter-of-fact. Just like on a typical night coming home from work.

We drove from the school to the border crossing at San Ysidro, passing taco stands and young men hawking everything from newspapers to fresh roses. Cielo was curled in a little ball under Linda's parka. She was quiet and still. It was as if she knew this was her only chance and wasn't about to blow it.

We jockeyed our way into the typically chaotic line of cars.

Traffic was light, and in minutes we were at the checkpoint. I recognized our border agent. He asked us the usual questions.

"Teaching, sir. Yes, teaching English at the Queen Elizabeth Institute. Yes, both my wife and myself. No sir, nothing to declare this evening."

It was a flawless performance. I was brilliantly normal. I had captured and portrayed that kind of day-after-day weariness that comes from crossing the border every day. And Cielo had fallen into nothing short of a coma. Not a squirm. Not a whimper. She knew the stakes.

My wife is the kind of person who always gives away the punch line of a joke at the very beginning of its telling. And then she always wants to start over again. So when the border guard asked Linda what was under her coat, my heart went into instant arrhythmia.

In a tone of voice that would best be described as that of the village idiot, she answered, "Oh, nothing. . . . Just my big feet."

My wife is a beautiful, graceful woman. So when the guard asked her to pick up her coat and she began acting like Elmer Fudd, I knew we were doomed. He asked her to step out of the car, walked around to the passenger side, and lifted up her coat. There he found our bearded little stowaway, fast asleep.

He said nothing about it. He asked us to get back in the car and tagged a very intimidating little piece of yellow paper to our windshield. He instructed us to proceed to Secondary Inspections, where agents have been known to completely dismantle cars and vans in minutes.

The yellow piece of paper said, "Hiding dog under coat." We were scared. Not so much for ourselves, but for Cielo. Even though she had found Linda only two hours earlier, she was already a part of us. We could not leave her behind.

One of my dreams when I moved to California was to hear the howl of a coyote. After dogs, they are my favorite animal. In Native legends, it is said that Coyote created the earth and carried fire down from the mountains. He was the mischief-maker, the trickster, and he could transform himself into any shape he wished. His ultimate responsibility, set down by the great Spirit Chief, was "to set things right," however he might interpret that mandate. Many of his best-laid plans and schemes didn't turn out the way he'd expected. At those times he used his trickery and cleverness to repair the situation. I thought of Coyote as we sat in that dimly lit holding area.

We waited about an hour. Finally, another border agent approached and asked us to step out of the car. She said very little—asked me to open the trunk. She poked around a bit with her flashlight and then plucked the yellow piece of paper from the windshield. She looked at it for a moment and with a wave of her hand told us to proceed across the border.

I don't think she heard a word of my story about how I had brought "Freckles" down to Mexico to show to my class as I talked about dog physiology. Just one look at Cielo and she would have known I was lying.

I have no idea why she let us go.

Maybe she recognized a gift from the sky.

from A SEARCH FOR THE PERFECT DOG

The Cat Who Came Home

JACQUELINE DAMIAN

I first set eyes on this cat just about nine years ago. It was mid-October, and there was a chill in the air that dark Friday night as an old boyfriend and I made our way from my grandmother's house in Massachusetts to my mother's place in Rhode Island. We hadn't eaten, so we decided to stop at a little Italian restaurant—the kind with paper plates and red-checkered plastic on the tables—in a group of shops off a rural stretch of road in Scituate, Rhode Island. We climbed the rough wooden steps to the walkway connecting the stores, only to find ourselves face to face with a small but self-assured black and white cat.

He sat upright on his haunches and fixed us with the wise, attentive gaze I would come to know well in the years that followed. (The ancient Egyptian word for cat, *mau,* also meant "to see," which is apt. Cats do stare, even if you're not always sure at what.) Even in the shadows you could see he was a handsome creature: a half-grown kitten, perhaps five or six months old, with a long, fluffy tail and an endearing white smooch on his nose. We stopped to pet him, of course—Sasha is one of those cats that seem to invite caresses—and then went inside to order.

When I came back out five minutes later to phone my mother and tell her I'd be late, there was Sasha, waiting at the door. He trotted behind me to the phone booth and rubbed sweetly around my ankles all the time I was talking, in an apparent attempt (successful, in the end) to insinuate himself in my affections. After I hung up he followed me back to the restaurant, and he looked very disappointed indeed when I closed the door in his face.

But Sasha is not one to be easily deterred. In a moment the door opened again as new customers came in, and Sasha hurtled in along with them. Blinking broadly for a moment as his eyes adjusted to the light, he scanned the restaurant until he spotted my companion and me. He then marched directly to our table.

By this time the two of us had begun discussing whether we should take the cat home. He was bewitching us, all right. But he didn't have the hallmarks of a stray—too clean and friendly, seemingly healthy, and apparently well fed. He must, I said, already have a home.

"Oh, no," replied our waitress, who materialized like a *deus ex machina* at just this critical moment. "That cat used to live at the house up the road, but the people there kept the mother and kicked out the kittens. He's been living out of our dumpster for a while now."

I chopped up one of my meatballs and put it on a plate to bring outdoors for the cat—who, the waitress said firmly, was not allowed to stay inside—and thought about what to do. At the time I already had two cats, and I knew the last thing these thirteen-year-old females wanted was a kitten in the house to harass them. They had protested in no uncertain terms the one time I brought home a stray, but luckily for all of us that obliging little calico seduced the electrician who was rewiring my kitchen at the time, and went happily home with him.

I picked up Sasha, took him and the meatball outside, and went back in to finish my meal and consider my options. No, I decided. Cute as he was, I couldn't take him home. I did not need another cat.

But when my companion and I left the restaurant a little while later, there was Sasha, waiting by the door. He had finished the meatball and looked up at us expectantly. What could be said in the face of the inevitable? My friend and I looked wordlessly at each other and opened the car doors as Sasha made his way down the stairs, pausing for a moment midway as if to ponder his future. He glanced back over his shoulder at the restaurant that had been his erstwhile home, then craned his neck to peer into the car. He looked back again, and again peeked into the car. Apparently having settled the matter to his own satisfaction, he jumped inside, climbed on my lap, and leaned hard against me in a kind of armless hug. He gave me a long, lovestruck look, heaved a big sigh, circled around in my lap, and settled down to sleep. The redoubtable Sasha had found himself a home.

from SASHA'S TAIL

"Make Yourself Comfortable, Rufus"

C. W. GUSEWELLE

---

*B*rilliance is a powerful asset. Wealth, if you're lucky enough to have it, can open some doors. But when it comes to getting ahead in the important things, patience is the sovereign virtue.

Take Rufus, for instance. He's about as bright as he needs to be, though you wouldn't call him a genius. And he's certainly not rich. But he has a clear idea of how he wants to live and is willing to advance toward his goal by measured stages.

In the beginning, as I've said, there was the doghouse. His destiny, it had been decided, was as an outdoor dog. He disagreed. Standing first on the roof of his house, and later on the patio table, he could look directly through a window and see the old dog, happy on her rug, and indoor people and a quantity of indoor cats. The logic of his being an outdoor dog escaped him. But there was a closed door between him and all that comfort, and he was small.

With bird dogs as with buffalo calves, however, the smallness is self-correcting. It just takes time. So he waited, and when his stature permitted he destroyed the door and came inside. Once in, he discovered that the old dog, the people and the cats spent their evenings in an upstairs bedroom. He was allowed to join them, provided he remained politely on the floor.

It did not escape his notice that the cats arranged themselves on the bed and, when the hour grew late, the people joined the cats and the old dog selected one of the people's soft chairs—chairs that for unfathomable reasons were forbidden him. He brooded for a time on this injustice. Then he realized that the people slept, and that what happened while they slept was unimportant to them.

If he was seen to be on the floor when the light went out, and again when the alarm sounded and the people stirred, he would be praised as a floor dog, not a chair dog. The quality of his nights improved. But the arrangement was limiting. Sometimes he liked to sleep in the daytime, too. Or in the evening hours before the people retired. So he began insinuating himself into the chair whenever it pleased him.

The people grew used to it. They learned to watch television sitting on footstools, while Cinnamon and the bird dog slept in the chairs.

There remained the issue of the bed. He leapt up there the first time barking an alarm, pretending to scare a burglar from the yard. Sometimes after that he sat on the bed to look through the window at rabbits among the flowers. When the people remembered they commanded him to get down. In time they remembered less often. Climbing the stair they would hear the thump of him leaving that unauthorized place. But when they came into the room he would be in his chair, the soul of innocence.

Seven years, it took, from the roof of the doghouse to the lap of comfort.

The other evening, in the middle of some program, the people happened to look at the bed and see him there, brazenly and in full view, curled in a knot as small as possible for a dog his size, trying to resemble a cat.

"Do you see it?" one of the people said.

His near eye was slitted open, looking at them looking at him. Then the eye slid shut in satisfaction.

So far, he still eats dog food and does not join them for meals at the table. But time is his ally, and he takes the long view. There's no sure way of knowing how far patience may get him or where ambition ends. But it's a pity to see what's happened to him. The tough, utilitarian beast has become a lounging fop, whose taste now runs to electric blankets set on 6.

from THE RUFUS CHRONICLE

The Fastest Dog on Earth

WILLIE MORRIS

He was a dog for all sports seasons. Ralph, the photographer in our group, once captured this quintessence in him, having him pose under the oak in my front yard with a St. Louis Cardinals baseball cap on his head, the lace of our football grasped between his teeth, his paw in a baseball glove, and in front of him on the grass a basketball, a baseball bat, four baseballs, my baseball spikes, a tennis racket, a volleyball, a football helmet, half a dozen or so sports magazines and game programs, and numerous baseball bubblegum cards.

I had even created a mythical dog football team of my own devising, consisting of various dogs I was familiar with in the town, and often when walking somewhere alone or riding on my bicycle I would entertain myself by reciting play-by-play accounts of games involving this team, which I called Kennel U. Using my mother's old Kodak camera, I went around taking snapshots of the dogs on the team, pasting them into the crude replica of an official game program, with thumbnail sketches of each dog, such as Sheriff Raines' Buck and the Hendrixes' Super-Doop. We operated out of the single-wing offense made famous by the Tennessee Volunteers. Skip was the tailback and, naturally, also the captain.

His dramatic touchdowns in our real football games in my front yard were fabled in the town, of course, but he also enjoyed watching the boys and me shooting baskets around the wooden basketball goal in back, and whenever someone made an errant shot that missed the entire backboard and bounced over the hedges toward the front, he would enthusiastically retrieve it and push it back to us with his nose. His swiftness and agility were likewise legend, and when of the spirit he could move so fast that I desired some specific authentication of his actual speed.

I borrowed Henjie's father's stopwatch one Saturday morning and persuaded some of the fellows to accompany us to the high school football field, where I intended to time Skip formally in the hundred-yard dash. The difficulty was that I knew I must improvise some method that would get him to race from one goal line to the other, exactly one hundred yards, at top velocity and in as straight a path as possible. How to do this? At first I had Henjie, Big Boy, and Peewee station themselves at the far goal line with the stopwatch while I positioned Skip at *our* goal line, in as close an approximation of the classic sprinter's stance before the starting gun as I could persuade him to assume. Then, on a signal from me, our three companions began shouting, *"Skip, come here!"* at which I would give him a vigorous shove to get him on the way. This did not prove efficacious, producing a series of false starts in which he might sprint fifteen yards in the right direction, or twenty, or twenty-five, then circle around and return to me. After a reflective conference the others and I arrived at the proper solution. Peewee would hold Skip at the starting line, with Big Boy and Henjie at the opposite line with the stopwatch. I would station myself at midfield and shout for Skip to follow me, then start running toward Big Boy and Henjie, and at that precise moment Peewee would release Skip, who would likely run after me in a straight line and at full acceleration for the entire distance.

This indeed worked perfectly the very first time we tried it. I yelled at him from the fifty-yard line and then began running in the opposite direction. The instant Peewee released him Henjie started the stopwatch. I ran as fast as I could, but in little time at all I could hear him approaching me from behind. I crossed the finish a mere three or four strides before he did. Then, with Peewee dashing alone down the field toward us in his keen curiosity, Big Boy and I approached Henjie, who had the stopwatch extended in his hand and was grinning with such wild felicity that I thought he might commence jumping up and down at any moment.

We looked at the stopwatch: *7.8 seconds!* Take into consideration if you will that the *human* world record in the hundred at that point in history was 9.4 seconds, held by a fellow named Mel Patton. I immediately surmised that the all-time world record for fox terriers was achieved on that day in this small-town high school football stadium of the American Southland. Who would have the audacity to question it? We did, after all, have four witnesses.

from MY DOG SKIP

Yes, Dogs Can Speak!

GLADYS TABER

$\mathscr{A}$ visitor asked me yesterday whether we could distinguish between the dogs by their barks. I looked at her with surprise, for it had never occurred to me that there should be a doubt about it. When you live with a bevy of dogs, you know that every one has a special way of phrasing things as well as a different tone of voice. We can even tell when an argument begins over a cherished bone whether we should drop everything and run, whether it is a diplomatic protest (and whoever takes those seriously?).

Holly, the Irish, has the widest range. A high, rusty squeak means, "Come quick, let me out [or let me in]." A deep contralto woof indicates that something strange is around, and what is it? This has a questioning lift at the end of it. Woof? A low bass rumble means that no paw should step near her bone or her dish. A long, pealing sound affirms the world is just too exciting, a person can hardly stand it. And finally there is a soft gentle murmuring in the throat which is purely conversational. This sound is inflected and rises and falls gently as long as I am willing to visit with her.

The cockers have their own vocabulary too, from the excited feminine tones of Jonquil to the sober measured bark of Especially Me when he sees a strange dog outside the fence.

Get along now, get along, he says with meaning, this is private property. Linda, the small black one, has a special bark for the laundry man, whom she dislikes with fervor. Even before the sound of his truck is heard, we know the laundry man is coming, for Linda begins to express herself. She never uses this particular bark on any other occasion.

In the night, if strange creatures seem to be around, Jonquil leads the whole chorus. She begins with a sharp, nervous bark which gradually rises into what I can only describe as a high soprano howl. It reminds me very much of some singers I have heard as they labor into those silly coloratura passages. There is something magical about this, for at once every other dog begins to howl too, accompanying her in baritone, bass, and Irish contralto. Once begun, the whole passage must go on to a definite end. As I turn on the light and wait for them to quiver into the last note, I wonder what dim racial memory rises in them? It is a ritual which must have developed far back in time, possibly when they communicated from wild hill to wilder valley. I do know this, Little Sister was always embarrassed by this performance, and held out as long as she could. Then she would give me an apologetic look and very softly join in. And when it was over, her dark muzzle would be laid on my lap and her eyes looked anxious. Silly performance, she indicated.

But Jonquil always looks smug. She has, she feels, taken care of a situation, although by now she has not, of course, the slightest notion of what started all this racket.

Just how long a dog remembers is a point of disagreement between me and the psychologists. Dogs remember better than most human beings. We had a small particolored cocker once who was a dedicated mother. One of her puppies went to a new home at eight weeks of age. Years later, the owners brought her back. As she came in the gate, Clover began screaming and jumping up and down, rushed over and began to wash her offspring's face. She was ecstatic the whole afternoon, wagging and skipping about. Now a four- or five-year-old dog cannot resemble an eight weeks' puppy, and Clover had had subsequent litters. Other visiting cockers left her indifferent, they were not her own. Her daughter remembered too that a bowl of warm milk should be in the back kitchen, and went directly there to check.

from STILLMEADOW SAMPLER

A Conspiracy of Cats

ROGER CARAS

*B*efore my daughter and her husband got their place up here near us in horse country, they owned a home on a quiet street in suburban Baltimore. Periodically, a pretty but fairly nondescript medium-coated cat appeared on their front porch or in the backyard. Eventually, she began coming into the house with the acknowledged resident cats, staying briefly only to eat or drink and even to nap a few times. She could be petted, even picked up, and was only slightly aloof. She seemed to be looking things over or thinking them through.

When my daughter checked around the neighborhood, several other families were having the same experience with the wanderer. She slept first in one house and then another, ate where she felt like eating, and was so pleasant that no one seemed to mind. Then one day she checked into my daughter and her husband's place carrying bag and baggage and that was that. She began using the inside cat box as her regular comfort station and showed no inclination to visit old friends up and down the block. She never left the house and yard again; and when it came time to move, Lilly, her family name now, went along. The new place is apparently fine with her, too.

Clearly, Lilly was checking out what the neighborhood had to offer, and she chose well. She is, by the way, a delightful cat.

When you see her curled up by the fire or on the foot of my granddaughter's bed or rubbing up against Fontine, the collie, or Zack, the Labrador retriever, purring, you have to grant her her survival skills.

I know of a more surprising case three thousand miles away in a very different world, Brentwood, just west of Beverly Hills. There has occurred a stunning victory for catkind.

Charlie and Jane Powell were children of Manhattan. They were both raised in the heart of New York City, in apartments, the children of two non-animal-oriented families, although they were culturally enriched in all other ways. There is nothing wrong with that (I guess), but it does create a kind of person who will very often stay in and repeat that mold.

Then came Mel, and it became evident that he would have to be an only child. Jane and Charlie, he a motion picture executive and she a book editor, were well read enough to know how much a pet was supposed to mean to a child, especially an only child; and although it was not a concept they knew by instinct or from firsthand experience, they decided to do what they were sure was right. Mel was to be denied nothing. With absolutely no more personal enthusiasm for the job than they would have experienced contracting a diaper service, they bought a puppy, an easy keeper for an apartment, a vest pocket-sized Yorkshire terrier, Little Nell. Before they quite realized what had happened they were in love, and deeply so. They did not feign amazement, they *were* amazed! As it turned out, they had both been closet animal lovers all along, without either of them having the remotest clue that he or she was carrying the bug. It was a joy to behold. Those of us who had grown up with animals just nodded knowingly and watched the pleasant scene unfold.

In good time the inevitable call from Hollywood came, and

the Powells with Mel and Nell in tow headed west. After Little
Nell met an unexpected and unhappy fate in a freak accident,
there was another Yorkie who managed to live out a good, full
life. Before a third dog could be selected, something happened
that changed everything. It was as unanticipated as their ado-
ration of Little Nell. Somewhere high in the clouds a finger or
perhaps a paw was pointed downward toward a beautiful
house in Brentwood, and the Powells were chosen.

Their very nice home with its swimming pool and mani-
cured gardens was being cased by a dark and handsome but
secretive stranger. Day and night, we must surmise, he who
was to become known as Seymour moved through their
shrubbery and among their flower beds. Seymour-to-be was a
black tomcat whose origins and early experiences are the
secrets of the gods of the cats and not knowable. Eventually,
Seymour let himself be seen and then he began to hang
around in the open near the patio. Well, the Powells reckoned,
the swimming pool water, full of chemicals as it always is,
can't be good for a cat, so a bowl, a cut-glass bowl, a once-
upon-a-time wedding present as I recall, was put out, and the
water was changed several times a day. A small enough comfort to offer a stranger perhaps from out of town.

Then one day Jane was shopping and passed the pet food
aisle in the supermarket. Why not? She bought the most expensive brand of cat food they had to offer and some toys.
Again, why not? So Seymour, now duly dubbed thus, was eating and drinking just outside the sliding patio doors. What happened next was inevitable. Someone en route to or from the
pool left a slider slightly ajar and Seymour the moocher stepped
inside never to leave again. He found a nicely puffed-up chair
with a pleasing view and settled in. Then came the cat box,
the litter, more toys, and a visit to the veterinarian. *Voilá!* The

Powells with renewed amazement realized they adored cats, too. They hadn't had even a clue, not a tic or a murmur before Seymour joined the family.

Seymour's arrival was even more remarkable than the Powells realized. For a cat to survive in that particular area is close to miraculous. In the surrounding hills and valleys there is a great deal of urban wildlife, including plenty of coyotes who love a good haunch of domestic cat for lunch. There are feral dogs, of course, but even worse for cats are the many estates that have guard dogs on patrol off lead. The Powells' home is only about four long city blocks north of Sunset Boulevard; and that wagon track is suicidal to cross in anything less than a tank and so, for that matter, are the avenues and streets that cross and feed into it. For Seymour to have spent any time at all as a wanderer in the Brentwood Westwood area and to have achieved his adulthood was amazing.

Before Charlie and Jane could totally understand what had happened to them, Katt appeared just as Seymour had. Katt is another jet black male cat and a very handsome beast, too. The only way he can be distinguished from Seymour is by his golden eyes. Seymour's are distinctly green. Heaven only knows where Katt came from or how he survived either, but there he is in the house living as high as Seymour is, both of them in peace and harmony. Some months later another cat I never met appeared, but quickly succumbed to what the veterinarian assured Charlie and Jane was a wholly intractable urinary disorder.

Then, suddenly, Arby appeared. She is a marmalade job, about the same size as the boys, and just as pleasant. They are all remarkable moochers. Before the Powells had quite understood that they owned three cats when neither of them had ever dreamed that they would own one, they somehow got shanghaied into a shelter and adopted their first kitten, a remarkable tortoiseshell named Moca.

Had word gotten around? Could there be an underground signal system that puts the news out, "Good pickings over on Homewood Way"? Or is it possible that cats really are watching that carefully and know or find out for themselves where the easy touches are to be found?

Several remarkable things have apparently occurred there in Brentwood. The cats, one at a time, for they came singly and spaced, picked the Powell household, although initially there was no odor of other cats to attract at least Seymour. They could not possibly have belonged to the estate's previous owner, because the Powells had been in place almost twenty years before cat number one fingered them. These cats are the descendants of wild, solitary creatures, and society does not come easily or naturally to them. Many domestic cats simply cannot share a home with other cats. Yet the Powell cats, obviously masters at adaptation, snuggle up with each other to sleep, share food dishes, bathe each other, and sit around and watch each other play with stuffed mice and myriad other toys. They have adjusted themselves perfectly to obtain and retain a luxurious lifestyle, not unlike that of the rich and famous.

There had to be a waiting and watching period with each of the three wanderers now on deck. They went shopping for people, found them, and converted them (relatively easy was the conversion of the family; it had already been demonstrated they are an easy mark), and made their oh so feline deal—beauty, love, and tranquility in exchange for a world of unending luxury and devotion. Cats play for high stakes, and the Powells have bought the package. All of this displays not only feline intelligence and adaptability but the cat's power to wait, watch, and select. Selectivity without observation is the wildest of wild gambling chances. Too often with cats it has been pick right or die.

My wife, Jill, and I were recently house guests in the feline manor in Brentwood; and the morning we left for the airport I called to Jane from the drive: "Arby is out here in the bushes."

"No, she's not. She's right here eating."

But there was a big marmalade cat out there, back in the bushes, just sitting and watching, and, I am sure, waiting. The Powells don't stand a chance.

from A CAT IS WATCHING

Bandit, the Fashion Hound

CRAIG WILLIAMS

I went to the humane society with specific instructions to find a small, short-haired female dog. Much to my wife's immediate chagrin, I returned with a medium-sized, long-haired male terrier and beagle mix. He was ridden with mange and ear mites, and had looked so woefully from the cage. He was next on the chopping block, a stray they had named Festus. We wound up calling him Bandit because he completely stole our hearts.

From a stray of unknown origin, Bandit has risen to CEO of a small law office, which he runs with a firm paw. He is known as the office fashion hound, wearing a different bow tie for each day of the week. After a long day at the office, Bandit needs a walk along the beach to unwind and socialize with his friends. After his grueling schedule, tummy rubbing is in order, and then it's off to bed, where he's gently tucked in and covered with his favorite "blanky."

While we've often wondered about Bandit's past, and what his life was like before we adopted him, we are certain of one thing—he is truly an angel sent to enrich our lives beyond measure.

from UNFORGETTABLE MUTTS

CARING WHEN IT COUNTS

"For it is in giving that we receive."

ST. FRANCIS OF ASSISI

Our animal friends have a special sensitivity to our needs. They can tell when we're troubled, lonely, disappointed, hurt or desperately in need. They also feel our joy, our excitement and our happiness. We don't have to say a word. They know. And they share all of these moments with us in their own way. When we need help, they give it wholeheartedly; when we're ready to play, they join in the fun. Sometimes they know we just need someone to sit quietly by our side and be there for us. It's their way of saying "I love you."

In time, we can learn to understand our best friends' needs almost as well. And when we do, we will experience that wonderful feeling of giving and helping that enables us to say, "I love you, too."

Doggy Baggage

ELEANOR GARRELL BERGER

I was a widow in my forties, sharing life with Photon, my thirteen-year-old miniature dachshund, when I met Mike. He was a bachelor, nice looking, my age, and a man my friends said came without baggage.

My friends, however, were wrong. They had overlooked Tycho, Mike's standard schnauzer. One look at Tycho, as he elegantly descended from the front seat of Mike's car, told me that on my driveway stood fifty pounds of doggy baggage. Not my choice for a pet. Tycho was too large. He looked too fierce. He needed grooming. And I could tell that his beard, an obvious dirt collector, was well designed for soaking up water from his bowl and dispensing it across my polished floors.

At first Tycho ignored me, preferring instead to sample unfamiliar scents along the driveway. As I approached Mike, however, he pranced over to inspect me. Positioning himself next to his master, like a chaperon at a dance, he whined his disapproval at our affectionate greeting. Photon, waiting just inside the door, yapped a few times. I glanced at Mike, then into the alert eyes on guard between us. My future was clear. The two of us were not going to forge a new relationship until the four of us formed a new pack.

Blended-dog families, like ours, have become common

today. Even dogless people may suddenly find themselves sharing a home with step-pets. These canines are different from puppies we select together and dogs we mutually adopt.

It was hard for me to accept Tycho. I tolerated him, even respected him, but didn't really like him until after he stayed with me for a week while Mike was out of town. I wasn't thrilled, but with only Photon for protection, a serious-looking dog seemed like welcome company. I was also thinking that Tycho and I might have a chance to connect without Mike in the picture. I was right.

One afternoon, while I worked in the garden and Tycho supervised, Photon, who had been sleeping in the sun, wandered off. Nearly blind, totally deaf, and mostly confused, he was incapable of finding his own way home. I left Tycho on a "down stay," and ran off in search of my lost dog. No Photon. Frantic and in tears, I returned to Tycho. Taking his muzzle in my shaking hands, I repeated a command he was hearing for the first time. "Find Photon. Find Photon."

I knew that Tycho had never retrieved anything in his life, and I felt foolish shouting at him. But I was scared, and he was all the help I had. He responded by tilting his head and staring at me. "Find Photon," I repeated. He remained still for a moment, and then moved off toward the woods. "Oh God," I thought. "Next, he'll disappear, and then I'll lose Mike, too."

A few minutes later I was startled to hear several snorts and to see a parade of dogs emerging from the woods. In the lead was blind little Photon, followed by Tycho, who occasionally tapped him from behind. I rushed over to hug Photon and then opened my arms to take in my step-dog. Tycho responded by rubbing and sighing and then braggingly prancing about. When he finally settled himself, he threw a look in my direction that said, "Okay, What's next?" I answered with another hug.

Now, when I look at Tycho, I no longer see fierce eyebrows and a messy beard. Instead, I see a dog I have learned to love, a cherished member of my family.

Sometimes, late in the evening, when Tycho is curling up, ready to fall asleep, I wait for him to look in my direction one more time. For when he does and his eyes meet mine, his look will say what we both are thinking: "Aren't we lucky Mike came with doggy baggage."

from OUR BEST FRIENDS

The Hippo and the Antelope

JEFFREY MOUSSAIEFF MASSON

In some extraordinary wildlife footage I was privileged to watch, a small impala antelope in Africa races away from a pack of wild dogs into a river where she is immediately seized by a large crocodile. Suddenly a hippopotamus rushes to the rescue of the dazed antelope. The crocodile releases his prey and the hippo then nudges the small animal up the bank of the river and follows her for a few feet until she drops from exhaustion. Instead of leaving, the hippo then helps the little creature to her feet and, opening his mouth as wide as possible, breathes warm air onto the stunned antelope. The hippo does this five times before returning to the forest. There is no possible explanation for this remarkable behavior except compassion.

from DOGS NEVER LIE ABOUT LOVE

A Little Girl Is Missing

SARAH WHALEY

"Mama, can we please keep Dog?" the girls begged for what was probably the fifteenth time that cold, gray January evening as they sat on the living room floor drawing. "Pretty please?"

I sighed. I had tried to make sure they didn't get too attached to the stray dog my husband, Alan, had brought home the week before. I hadn't allowed them to name him or even bring him inside. But from the minute the little beagle had scrambled from the back of their daddy's truck into their arms, six-year-old Elizabeth and three-year-old Amanda had fallen in love with him. Out by Alan's workshop they had turned a cardboard box into a doghouse, complete with a crayoned window and a musty blanket for a bed.

"We can't keep him," I reminded my daughters, "even if his owner doesn't turn up. But don't worry, we'll find him a good home." I couldn't bear to look at their crestfallen expressions, so I glanced at the pictures they were drawing. Wouldn't you know it? There was the beagle again.

With those long, floppy ears and big chocolate eyes, he was cute all right. But I knew he would be more trouble than he was worth. He was already sending our cats scurrying, and as soon as the ground thawed in the spring he would dig up the yard, or, worse, the wheat and bean fields Alan's dad farmed on our property. No, the girls and the household were enough. I didn't need a dog to look after too.

Alan had a soft spot for dogs. From time to time he found strays, or as he put it, they found him. The weekend before, the beagle had trotted up to him, wearing a collar but no tag. "He was real friendly," Alan told me. "He jumped into the back of my truck like he wanted to come home with me, and, well, what could I do?"

Now, of course, it's up to me, I thought as I put away the supper dishes. Since no one had called to claim the dog, I was going to have to find a home for him—fast.

The wind rattled the windows, and I shivered, glad to be inside. I'd have to bundle the girls up when I put them to bed. I couldn't wait to get some shut-eye myself. I had been on my feet since before dawn, working my shift at a local tool factory.

But first there were chores to finish. I dragged the vacuum cleaner out of the closet, wondering if I would ever be able to keep up with everything. It all seemed so overwhelming sometimes.

Alan came in from his workshop. A chill breeze sneaked in the front door after him, but Elizabeth and Amanda didn't seem to mind. They ran to him, hugging him around the knees. "Do you think Dog's warm in the house we made him?" Elizabeth asked.

"He might be," Alan said. "Or he might be curled up in a nice spot under my shop. Either way, he'll be okay." I hid a smile. Except for sniffing the box politely when the girls had first shown it to him, the dog hadn't shown any interest in it. Alan was just too sweet to say so.

He played with Elizabeth and Amanda while I finished vacuuming. Then it was bedtime. The girls put on their pajamas. They said their prayers (asking to keep the dog, I'm sure) and scooted into their beds. "Good night," I murmured, tucking their covers snugly around them. "Sleep tight."

I hoped they would. Usually they woke and ended up crawling into our bed in the middle of the night. I felt so wiped out that night I didn't think I would even notice. I slid into bed gratefully, and as always I said a quick prayer: *Lord, watch over our girls.*

When I opened my eyes it was morning. Looking out the window as I sat up and stretched, I could see it was the kind of raw winter morning when the sun barely breaks through the mist that sits on the fields like a heavy blanket.

Elizabeth was beside me, sound asleep, but for once Amanda wasn't in her spot between Alan and me. I got up and peeked in her room. Her covers were in a big lump in the middle of the bed. I smiled. My smart girl must have wiggled herself into a toasty cocoon and slept through the night in her own bed.

Did she? I thought with a sudden stab of concern. Amanda was such a restless sleeper, and the covers seemed so still. Gently I pulled them back. The bed was empty. "Alan," I called, puzzled, "where's Amanda?"

He met me in the hallway. "Hon, she isn't in our room," he said, looking a little worried. "You think she's on the couch?" We both headed to the living room.

That's when I saw the front door. Wide open. But the storm door on the outside was shut tight. "Oh, no!" I gasped. Alan and I stared at each other in dismay. Amanda could open both doors from the inside, but from the outside she couldn't possibly reach the handle on the storm door, even from the top step, to let herself back in.

We checked the house quick, just to be sure. She wasn't anywhere. *My baby spent the night in the pitch dark, chilled to the bone and scared out of her wits? She must have been crying for Mama and Daddy to come and get her.* I felt like crying, but I knew I had to focus. *Amanda's out there somewhere freezing, and we've got to find her!*

Alan and I rushed outside. The wind stung my cheeks. What hope was there for a three-year-old alone all night in this cold?

I wanted to scream my prayer to make sure God heard me, but all I could manage was a whisper: "Please help us find her!"

"I'll take the back," Alan said. "You check the front." We went in opposite directions, calling Amanda's name. No sign of her in the carport. I ran across the drive to Alan's workshop. Maybe she had seen the light he left on and had tried to get in there.

"Amanda!" I yelled. The wind seemed to carry her name away. "Where are you?"

Then I heard a tiny sound. A whimper? I listened carefully. Something brushed my leg. But it was only the beagle, standing in the light coming from Alan's shop. He looked at me, then back over his shoulder at the house the girls had made for him. The box was caved in from snow and ice.

He just wants to come inside. I started to walk away. Then I heard the sound again. I went back. The dog hadn't moved from his place beside the box. He stood, feet planted stubbornly, and stared right at me, an insistent look in his eyes.

"What are you trying to tell me, boy?" I asked. He cocked his head and glanced toward the box again.

I dropped to my knees and stuck my head inside. Amanda! She was huddled in the corner, her eyes glassy. "Alan, I found her!" I shouted, pulling my baby to me. Alan took her and ran to the house.

We layered her in warm clothing and wrapped her in a quilt. Amanda was shaking violently, and we couldn't get a reading on the thermometer. Alan's dad came over to watch Elizabeth. We sped to the hospital, where doctors started emergency procedures.

After getting fluids by IV for a few hours Amanda began to come around. She was going to be all right. Nothing more than mild hypothermia, dehydration and a little windburn on her chubby cheeks. "Oh, Honey," Alan said, hugging her close, "why in the world did you go out in the middle of the night?"

Amanda wasn't sure. When she woke up she found herself wandering around outside the house. The dark scared her, so she knocked on the door. When we didn't answer she went to her daddy's shop, but it was locked. Somehow she ended up getting in the box, and the beagle got in too, snuggling up next to her and keeping her from freezing. "It was okay, Mama," Amanda insisted. "Dog was with me the whole time."

Someone else had been with her that cold winter's night, someone who watches over us lovingly and protectively, the way we watch over our children. I still work hard to take care of my family, including its newest member, the loyal beagle Amanda named Lucky. It's a little easier now, though, knowing God is always looking after us too.

The Noble Dog

GEORGE GRAHAM VEST

---

*G*entlemen of the Jury: The best friend a man has in this world may turn against him and become his enemy. His son and daughter that he had reared with loving care may become ungrateful. Those who are nearest and dearest to us, those whom we trust with our happiness and our good name, may become traitors to their faith. The money that a man has he may lose. It flies away from him when he may need it most. Man's reputation may be sacrificed in a moment of ill considered action. The people who are prone to fall on their knees and do us honor when success is with us may be the first to throw the stone of malice when failure settles its cloud upon our head. The only absolutely unselfish friend a man may have in this selfish world, the one that never deserts him, the one that never proves ungrateful or treacherous is his dog.

A man's dog stands by him in prosperity and poverty, in health and sickness. He will sleep on the cold ground, when the wintry winds blow and the snow drives fiercely, if only he can be near his master's side. He will kiss the hand that has no food to offer, he will lick the wounds and sores that come in encounter with the roughness of the world. He guards the sleep of a pauper as if he were a prince.

When all other friends desert, he remains. When riches

take wings and reputation falls to pieces he is as constant in his love as the sun in its journey through the heavens. If fortune drives the master forth an outcast into the world, friendless and homeless, the faithful dog asks no higher privilege than that of accompanying him to guard him against danger, to fight against his enemies, and when the last scene of all comes, and death takes his master in its embrace and his body is laid away in the cold ground, no matter if all other friends pursue their way, there by his graveside will the noble dog be found, his head between his paws and his eyes sad, but open in alert watchfulness, faithful and true even to death.

The Woman in Apartment 23-C

ELLEN SECREST

I jumped out of the car and ran up the front steps of the old apartment house. It was my turn to deliver a hot meal to the elderly woman in Apartment 23-C. She was very sweet, very lonely and loved to chat, but I never gave her a chance to say anything.

You see, this woman was fond of cats and shared her tiny apartment with six adored felines. The problem was litter boxes. There just weren't enough of them to handle this household. So each time I stepped inside her door, I smiled, put the lunch tray down on the nearest table and made a rapid retreat—holding my breath until I got back into the hall.

Then one day, I heard a story about an old rabbi who asked his students how they knew when nighttime had ended and the new day had begun. One pupil thought it happened when one saw an animal in the distance and was able to tell whether it was a sheep or a dog. Another guessed that it happened when one looked at a tree in the distance and could tell whether it was a fig tree or a peach tree. The wise rabbi shook his head at both of these answers.

"Then how can you tell when night has ended?" the students asked.

"You can tell when you look at the face of any human being and see that he is your brother or sister. If you cannot do this, then it is still night."

The next time I visited the old woman's apartment I lingered for a little while. Her smile and the light that came into her eyes made the place bearable. Shortly after, a group of us contacted a local social services agency, explained the situation and made arrangements for weekly housecleaning to be done. Now she is living with the cats she loves in a healthy environment—and I'm taking the time to get to know her better.

The Undercover Cat

CLEVELAND AMORY

here was a reason Polar Bear was at the hospital. Marian, who could not visit me that day, had a friend bring Polar Bear down in his carrier to see me. The friend was supposed to return before visiting hours were over and take Polar Bear back, but unfortunately an emergency came up and she could not make it. Since that particular day and night the other bed in the two-bed room was unoccupied, I decided that if Polar Bear spent the night he would at least not be bothering anybody else. I even took the precaution of spreading some newspaper in the bathroom for a serviceable litterbox. . . .

I did, however, have a serious talk with Polar Bear. I told him that during the night an almost steady stream of people would be passing through our room because that is the way hospitals work—they were sort of like railroad stations. Furthermore, I warned him, most of the people who would be passing in or through the room would be dressed in white, but he would not in any circumstance regard them as veterinarians. Indeed, I told him, he was not to regard them at all because I wished him, from the moment he heard footsteps approaching outside the door, to get under the covers and stay there without leaving in view even so much as one of his beady eyes.

I could tell by his tone of listening—and do not fool yourself, Polar Bear did indeed have a tone of listening—that he did not go along with my idea about this. Clearly, he wanted to know that if this was how it was going to be in the hospital, how in the world could I expect him to do his job of protecting me?

There are all kinds of protection, I told him sternly, just the way there are those who also serve who only stand and wait. They also protect, I added to make it absolutely clear, who only lie and wait. But lie and wait, I added firmly, was just what I expected him to do.

I next told him our first trouble would be the arrival of my supper. The minute I said "supper," Polar Bear could not see what trouble that could possibly be. I explained that it would be trouble because it would probably be brought by a man or a woman in white, and before he started to jump out of bed and up on the tray it would be nice if he at least waited until the man or woman had put the tray down.

I was of course being sarcastic. I didn't want under any condition for him to appear until the man or woman in white had left not only the tray, but also the room.

Polar Bear had the clearest way of asking, "And where, may I ask, do I come in?" The way he did it was by coming as close as a cat can to a cocked eyebrow. I told him he came in because the minute the man or woman went, then and only then could he come out and share my supper. And amazingly enough, it all happened exactly as we discussed it. The minute I heard the wheels of the meal cart outside the door I swooped Polar Bear under the covers and the man came in, put down the tray, and left, all so quickly that Polar Bear did not have time to do anything about it. Once we were alone, however, out he came, and dove for the supper tray. And so, between us, as we so often did at home, we shared and shared alike, his idea of sharing and sharing alike being that he ate both his share and my share of what he liked and left me to have both my share and his share of what he did not like.

When we were through I again placed him under the covers until the man had come in and removed the tray. Afterwards, I warned Polar Bear that we were far from out of the woods yet. Still to come, I told him, were at least three more visits. I also told him that, from then on, one or the other of us should stay awake and that we should schedule watches the way they do on shipboard. Since by this time Polar Bear was already yawning his head off—which was a tendency he often had when I was starting on something important—I decided to teach him a lesson and told him I would take the first shift from ten to twelve, and he could then take what I explained to him was the beginning of the graveyard shift, from twelve to two, and then again I would take over from two to four. There were only two troubles with this beautifully thought-out plan of mine. For one thing, we did not have an alarm clock, and for another we did not know exactly what our battle plan would be when the one who was on watch called the other to action. Actually, Polar Bear was terrific at waking me when he wanted something, but I had no idea how good he would be at waking me when he did not want something or wanted something to stop.

Anyway, we were in the middle of all these plans when suddenly I heard footsteps and the door opened and we had our first visitor. She turned on the light, moved swiftly to my bed, and put down a tray with some water and a pill in a cup. "It's our medication," she said. So far she had not even looked at me or the bed and I was sure she had not seen Polar Bear. But now she was turning and would see Polar Bear. Polar Bear, however, was nowhere to be seen. He was back under the covers. What he had done of course was to see the pill—and all I can say is that if I have ever seen a cat show the white feather I saw it then. I knew perfectly well how Polar Bear felt about pills, but this was too much. When it was all over and he came out, I had to explain to him what showing a white feather meant. I told him that it was plain and simple cowardice. He wanted to know where it came from, and I told him never mind where it came from, he would not remember it anyway. Actually, I learned it came from the belief that a gamecock with a white feather in his tail would not be a good fighter, and I did not see any reason for bringing up such a sordid subject as cockfighting.

I really gave him a very good speech, but the last part of it fell upon deaf ears. He had fallen asleep again. This of course I could not permit. It was now his watch, and people who went to sleep on their watch were often shot. Also I told him I particularly did not want him to go to sleep again before the sleeping pill nurse came—because sleeping pill nurses get very angry when patients go to sleep on them before they have had a chance to give them their pills. I informed Polar Bear sternly I simply would not answer for the consequences if the sleeping pill nurse saw him under such circumstances—it would be bad enough if she saw him under normal circumstances.

Once more I dozed off, and once more it seemed only a short time before the door opened again and this time the lights came flooding on as well as the cheerful question, "How are we tonight?" All I could do was reply wanly that I was as well as could be expected. Once more there was, of course, no Polar Bear in evidence. He was under the covers again, sleeping on picket duty—really he was impossible—particularly since we were this time faced with the temperature-and-pulse nurse. First she put the thermometer in my mouth and then reached for my wrist. This was a mistake. Polar Bear almost in-variably took exception to strangers attempting intimacies with me. Out came, all too visibly, one of his arms with its paw headed ominously for the nurse's hand. I had a brief thought that what we would now have would be a three-person arm wrestle, but unfortunately the situation was far worse than I thought. The nurse could not fail to see Polar Bear's arm ap-pear from under the covers, but that was not the main trouble. The main trouble was that she did not think the arm belonged to a cat. What she thought it belonged to was far worse—she thought it belonged to a snake. In any case she shrieked her displeasure, jumped up and made a mess of everything, in-cluding the thermometer in my mouth.

At this juncture I could hear steps coming down the hall—probably, I thought, the nurses' guard. Immediately I took the thermometer out of my mouth and reached under the covers where, good as gold, Polar Bear still was. I pulled him out and held him up, in all his glory, for the nurse to see. See, I said, no snake, no snake at all, just a dear little cat.

By this time she did not know what to think, but it was Polar Bear who saved the day. He did not hiss at her or do any-thing threatening, but instead gave a definitive purr and then one of his perfected silent AEIOU's. It won her over in an instant—in fact, before her nurses' guard appeared, she had actually helped me to get Polar Bear back under the covers. By the time they marched in I was having both my temperature and pulse taken as if nothing had happened.

from THE BEST CAT EVER

Sky-High With an Eagle

JOHN STOKES

was waiting in the director's office of the large metropolitan zoo where I worked as an assistant curator. The director walked in, sat at his desk and got right to the point. "John, we're not in the business of doing sideshows with a disabled bird," he said emphatically. "I'm sorry, but this Osceola thing of yours has gotten out of hand."

I wanted to interrupt right then and remind him how far that one-winged bald eagle had come since someone had found him nearly dead two years earlier, his left wing blown apart by a poacher's gunshot, how popular he had become with the crowds that visited the eagle exhibit and what an education he had offered the public about this tragically endangered species. But it was my boss talking so I kept still.

"Find a new home for Osceola," he said. "That's an order."

I suppose he had a point. Our zoo was for healthy animals, and Osceola required some extra work. But on that hot day in 1984, I didn't want to hear all that. In my mind the message was clear: *Listen, kid, you and that one-winged bird can just hit the road! Scram!*

The work I did at the zoo combined my two abiding pas-

53

sions in life—animals and flight. Growing up, I earned the nickname "Bird Boy." One reason was my fascination with all feathered creatures, whether it was Green Sam, my pet parakeet, or a clutch of orphaned starlings in the garage. The other was my singular determination to fly, which I first attempted when I was five by leaping off an old sweet gum tree with a bedsheet parachute stuffed into one of my mama's big leather handbags. Fortunately a branch broke my fall.

By the time I hit my twenties I was an accomplished hang-glider pilot. The one-man glider, from which the pilot hangs in a harness underneath the kitelike superstructure, was as close as I could get to genuine avian flight without sprouting a pair of wings. Circling a couple of thousand feet above the earth gave me an incredible rush of freedom, peace and beauty. My problems, like the ground below, seemed to slip away. I lived for that feeling.

But as I left the director's office and stormed back to Osceola's cage that day, life's troubles seemed to smash me to the ground. I was trying to get over a painful divorce. I couldn't afford to quit my job, yet I didn't want to be separated from Osceola, who felt like my one true friend. *Lord, what am I going to do?* I prayed, more as a lament than an actual question. That's why I was surprised to sense an answer immediately: *Have faith. I will show you.*

Show me what? I wondered, plucking a herring from a pail and feeding it to Osceola. He looked at me sharply as if to say, "Hey, what's up?" and I fed him another herring, wondering if he would be able to handle the move.

Al Cecere, a filmmaker who had recently formed the National Foundation to Protect America's Eagles (NFPAE), helped me find a home for Osceola at a predator rehabilitation-center in Nashville, Tenn., several hundred miles away. I kept working my zoo job, visiting Osceola whenever I could. I wanted to marry the woman I was seeing, but she called it off. *Another failed relationship,* I thought. I couldn't help wondering why my life seemed to go in circles.

My only relief besides work was hang gliding high above the earth, where eagles fly. *Like Osceola used to,* I thought one day as I drifted on a lazy thermal, turning a slow spiral in the sky. It made me profoundly sad to think that because of his amputated wing Osceola could never experience the unbounded joy of flight again.

Or could he?

The inkling of an idea began to form. I had once heard of a man who had developed a slinglike arrangement to take his dog hang gliding with him. At the time it struck me as a little crazy but admirable. Could I do something similar for Osceola? *He would love that.* It was just an idea, but someday . . .

With the help of funds Al Cecere managed to raise, the rehab center was able to hire me, and I moved to Nashville in the spring of 1986, taking a drastic cut in pay but ecstatic to be reunited with Osceola. I also got to work designing a hang-gliding harness for Osceola. "Don't worry, old bird," I told him, "someday you're going to fly again."

The rehab center was barely staying afloat. Pretty soon I found myself in charge of it, a mixed blessing if ever there were one. There was nothing in the bank. To save on gas I bicycled five miles to work on a busy road. A sympathetic friend gave me a gross of green beans and peas, and one morning I was reduced to eating peas and beans for breakfast. It had come to that!

Later that day I did some serious praying while sitting on a rock in the brush behind the center. I was dead broke. My dream of taking Osceola aloft was in jeopardy; I barely had money to feed myself, let alone to go hang gliding. "God, up in the sky, close to you I'm fine. But down here on earth troubles just seem to pile up. If something doesn't happen soon I'm going to have to shut this place down and move in with my mother!" Just as before, a response formed in my mind: *Hold on. Something is about to happen.*

A couple of seemingly little things did. The center got a financial shot in the arm from a sympathetic donor. And Al Cecere called and offered to hire me and give Osceola a home. "John, I have this vision of an eagle center on a mountainside. It would include a breeding-and-rehabilitation facility as well as educational programs. I'm trusting God will open the door for us."

I had been trusting for a while now. My tank was empty and I was running on spiritual fumes. Al and I displayed birds outside shopping malls and in local schools, giving talks about the endangered bald eagle and collecting donations one hard dollar at a time. Then misfortune struck again. I fractured my left arm in a hang-gliding accident. I couldn't help thinking how it was Osceola's *left* wing that had been amputated. "Maybe flying days are over for both of us now, buddy," I told him. Still, when I prayed, I sensed a response: *Something big is about to happen.* But when? How?

By spring of 1990 my arm had healed and I was hang gliding again, getting my tattered confidence back. Al had had a brainstorm. A friend, country singer James Rogers, was performing at Dollywood, entertainer Dolly Parton's theme park in Pigeon Forge, Tenn. James helped Al get a meeting with the folks at the park, where he pitched the idea of an eagle exhibit and center, complete with daily birds-of-prey shows featuring— you guessed it—Osceola and me. Before I had a chance to tell him what a long shot the idea was, the folks at Dollywood were offering to build the NFPAE an eight-hundred-thousand-dollar facility, including an eagle aviary, on a mountainside, just as Al had envisioned!

Something big certainly *had* happened, so big it couldn't have happened without God. Nine months later Al and I, 20 eagles including Osceola, along with assorted owls and hawks, moved to the Great Smoky Mountains—all part of the Wings of America bird show and Eagle Mountain Sanctuary, the largest eagle exhibit in the country. We were blessed with success almost immediately. Then, just as my life finally attained some stability, along came another whirlwind. Her name was Vikki; she was a singer in one of the other shows. *Oh, no,* I thought. *I know where this will lead.* Again, though, I heard the inner voice: *Hold on a minute. This will be different.*

It was. In 1994 Vikki and I were married. Things were finally coming together in my life. One more prayer remained to be answered. *Lord, I am so grateful for all you have given me. Please help us find a way for Osceola to fly again.*

By February of 1996 I finally came up with a safe and workable harness. Then we had to get Osceola accustomed to the strange contraption. People sure did gawk when we drove a pickup truck around and around the Dollywood parking lot carrying a mounted hang glider with a man and an eagle slung under it.

On a cool April morning in 1996 Al and I drove to the local hang-gliding airstrip, where we unloaded the glider and Osceola in his travel kennel. Doubts and prayers skirmished in my head as the hang glider was attached to a towline behind an ultralight plane that would take us aloft. I strapped myself into my harness while Al placed Osceola into his, secured it on a reinforced metal bar and clipped him to my harness. "Today, you're going to fly again, buddy," I told him. Al put his hand on my helmet and said a quick prayer. We were ready.

The ultralight revved its engine and we got a rumbling, rolling start. Osceola struggled a bit, startled by the motion. *Easy, buddy. Easy.* As we lifted off and gained altitude, though, Osceola relaxed. At 2000 feet I released from the towline. The buzz of the engine faded as I banked into a calm wind. We were flying.

I saw Osceola's head was bent slightly downward, moving deliberately from side to side. I followed his gaze. He was tracking a couple of hawks flying 100 feet or so below us. Thirteen years had passed since he had been able to peer down on the lesser birds of the air. Maybe I was projecting human feelings onto him but I could swear I saw something like a spark of regal pride in Osceola's piercing golden eyes.

An incredible sensation of warmth swelled my chest. I pulled into a slow turn, catching a thermal and spiraling upward gradually. I knew then my life hadn't been traveling in circles but in a spiral, ever higher day by day, drawn closer by faith to God.

The Case of the Lonely Swan

GARY RICHMOND

When I was at the zoo, the phone in the health center rang one day and the senior keeper of the bird section asked if we could take a look at a female coscoroba swan. These are rare swans, smaller and more delicate than their larger cousins. He told us that the other workers in that section had noticed that her ability to walk was deteriorating. Now she could only stumble a few steps before toppling forward into the mud at the edge of the zoo lake.

When we arrived at the lake we saw those very symptoms. Our veterinarian, Dr. Bernstein, who was an excellent vet, said, "I'm not prepared to make a diagnosis until we've done some testing." The bird keepers caught her and put her in a gunnysack. Her head and neck slid through a hole in the bottom, but her body was snug and comfortable inside the bag for the ride to the health center. She could not thrash around and injure herself while in the sack.

The male coscoroba swan to whom she was pairbonded was beside himself and didn't know how to defend her. He stayed in the water offshore and honked and whistled as we drove away. I noticed that the female had her eyes fixed on him all the way to the truck, and she answered his cries with some of her own. It was a sad parting. "We'll try to get you home as soon as possible, sweetheart," I said as she cried on the way to the health center.

We tried every test known to man but could not form an honest theory explaining why the swan could not walk. We did blood work, looked for bruises, and X-rayed her, but the tests only served to frustrate us because they didn't provide any clues. The swan frustrated us even more by refusing her food. I put her in a tub of hot water daily to help the circulation in her legs and rubbed them down for the same reason.

Day after day we watched her decline. There didn't seem to be any particular reason for it. She looked so sad. Most of the time she just lay quietly with her head turned to the wall and her neck curved so that she looked terribly depressed. One day Dr. Bernstein said, "Boys, she looks lonely. Swans mate for life, don't they?"

"Yes," I answered, anticipating what he was going to say.

Sure enough, Dr. Bernstein said, "Call the bird section and ask them if they could catch the male coscoroba for us. I think she could use a little company. I bet that's why she went off her feed."

I called the bird section just as they were getting ready to call me. They said that the male was on a hunger strike too, most likely protesting the removal of his mate. They asked if they could bring him up to the center.

The reunion was classic. As soon as they saw each other they began honking and whistling and started a head-and-neck bobbing ritual that I assume was a way of reestablishing their bond. In no time they were lying next to each other, eating like they had never eaten before. The female immediately began to improve. Two weeks later she was normal.

from IT'S A JUNGLE OUT THERE

Something More Important

PHYLLIS HOBE

---

*O*ne evening, a few months ago, I was taking my dog for a late walk. Our route was along a quiet country road, with no houses on either side, only fields and woods. "Hurry up, Suzy!" I said whenever she stopped to sniff. It was getting dark, and I wanted to go to the library before it closed.

Finally, I decided we had gone far enough. "Let's go home," I said, turning around. But Suzy kept facing in the other direction. "Come!" I said, using a command that always gets results. Suzy didn't budge. She looked back at me, and even in the twilight I could see concern in her eyes.

From the fields around us, where the grass was waist high, I heard a high-pitched sound. I thought it might have been a bird, and when Suzy pulled in that direction, I went along with her. The grasses parted, and a tiny, black and white kitten stumbled toward us, crying pitifully. It was skinny and dirty, its face scratched by thorns. Suzy bent down to lick its head as if to reassure it. I picked up the kitten and carried it home, where it was only too happy to eat and fall asleep curled up next to Suzy. That scruffy kitten has now grown into a healthy, handsome cat named Dennis, who gives our family lots of joy.

On that first night I was disappointed because I was out so late that I couldn't go to the library. But God had something more important that He wanted me to do—and I've always been thankful that He helped me to stop and listen to His plan.

Second Puppyhood

ALEXANDER CAMERON

One day an elderly couple came into the surgery with their Labrador dog, which was also elderly.

"It's his eyes," they said, something that was at once obvious for they looked terrible. I lifted the old dog on to the table and had a look at them. Both eyes were filled with pus, they were half closed, and the dog kept blinking and pawing at them.

"How long has he been like this?" I asked.

"Oh, he's been bothered with them for a long time, and we've had him to a vet several times before. He gave us ointment to put in them, but we've just retired to Bristcombe and they seem to have gone worse."

"Did your other vet tell you what the trouble was?"

"He just said it was inflammation, conjugal, or conjunction or some name like that," they explained.

"Well, his eyes are certainly inflamed, but I'm afraid no ointment will put them right. You see, it's more than conjunctivitis, he's got a condition called entropion where the eyelashes grow inwards and irritate the eyes, then germs get in, and cause all this matter. It's a very painful condition, like having something in your eye all the time, only worse."

"Oh dear! Can anything be done?" asked the wife.

"Certainly! There's a quite simple little operation which can turn the eyelashes outwards and take away the irritation."

"An operation!" they both gasped in unison.

"Oh, it's quite a little one, and it would make all the difference to him. What's his name, by the way?"

"Terence!" said the wife, and at the sound of his name, the old dog's tail beat a tattoo on the table.

"Couldn't you just give us ointment like the other vet?" asked the husband. "You see, he's old to have an operation."

"Yes, I could give you ointment, but it would not cure the condition, only soothe his eyes a little for a time. I strongly advise you to let me do the operation. It would take away all the pain, make his eyes clear again, let him see properly, for he's really a handsome old fellow, and it's a pity to see him like that."

"Would it be safe?"

"Yes! It means an anaesthetic, of course, and there's always a very slight risk with an anaesthetic, but it's maybe 1 in 1000. I'll just sound his heart," which I did, and got a fine, strong, regular beat.

"Sound as a bell, Mr and Mrs . . . eh?"

"Murgatroyd," said the man.

"Er . . . how much would such an operation cost?" he asked.

"Oh . . . about three guineas."

"Oh . . . is that all," said the old chap. "What do you think, Celia?"

"I don't know, Cyril, but if he was going to be operated on, I'd want to be there. I think we should both be there."

"Oh, I wouldn't advise that," I hastily exclaimed. "Most people get upset to see their animals being operated on. There's bound to be a little blood, you know."

So they talked to and fro, finally decided on surgery, but

only on condition that they could stay with their "dear old fel-low." I did not like the idea one bit, but for the dog's sake, agreed. Our operation day, apart from emergencies, was Wednesday, so Terence Murgatroyd was duly fixed up for 11.00 am, the next week. I decided I had better take some precautions, so Mrs Drury, our original Secretary/Receptionist/Assistant/Book-keeper, who was with us in my early years with Kenneth as partner, was despatched to lay in a bottle of brandy for the surgery, and two chairs were placed in position, a bit from the table, on the morning of the operation. The dog was lifted onto the table, and I cleaned up his eyes, then explained to Cyril and Celia the procedure to be adopted with Terence.

"First I give him an injection of anaesthetic into a vein, and he will just go quietly to sleep. . . . Perhaps you would find it more comfortable to sit down to watch."

But they did not. Mrs M in particular, a stout woman, wanted a close up, and her small husband, not to be outdone also hovered nearby, so four heads were bent over the now re-cumbent Terence. The operation is not difficult, but requires care and concentration, and I was wrapped up in what I was doing, as was Mrs Drury, constantly swabbing the area, when after a short time, I heard a faint voice saying, "It's awful warm today!" and engrossed as I was, it took a moment to sink in. When it did, I turned quickly to say "sit on the chair," but I was too late. There was a mighty crash and I was just in time to see large Mrs Murgatroyd sit down on the floor, right on top of her little husband who had tried to catch her, both of them missing the chairs. The little man peered out from underneath and murmured, "My wife appears to have fainted!"

I had seen many people faint at surgery, even big husky farmers watching a Caesarean in their sheep, but never quite a situation like this. There was nothing for it but to suspend operations, and while Mrs Drury and I eased the wife up, for her husband's ribs would be in dire peril, the little man crawled out from underneath, like a tortoise coming out of its shell. Between us we carted the unconscious lady into the Waiting Room, and not without difficulty, deposited her on the couch. Mrs Drury produced the brandy, and since poor little Cyril looked as if he was about to faint too, gave him a little, then left him sitting beside his wife, lying in a heap on the couch, her hat askew.

"Best just to leave her as she is," I said (I didn't really know!), "and when she comes round, perhaps a little sip of brandy." Poor Cyril nodded, and Mrs Drury and I left him patting his wife's hands as we trooped back to our patient.

In due course the operation was finished, just in time, for with the interruption, the effects of my short-acting anaesthetic were wearing off. . . . We lifted the old dog down, laid him on a blanket, then hurried through to see the other patient. She was a little bit ahead of Terence, being able to sit up, though pale, and with the hat even more askew, her eyes a bit glazed, and a glass of brandy in her hand, she would hardly have qualified at that moment for a temperance advert! Cyril, I noticed, was also at the brandy again, and I thought the profit from the operation had already been drunk! We were able to cheer Mrs M up a bit by telling her Terence had come through his surgery well, and when they were ready, we would carry him out to the car and they could take him home.

They returned in ten days to have the stitches removed, and this time they both stayed in the Waiting Room. I was agreeably surprised at the improvement already in the old dog's eyes, the chloromycetin twice daily allied to the removal of the irritation having worked wonders. They came back a fortnight later, and it was lovely to behold. Terence was frisking along like a young dog, looking about him everywhere. I imagine it was a long time since he had seen the world properly, but he was seeing now alright, and had a lot of catching up to do. His eyes were clean and bright as a puppy, a complete transformation.

from POULTRY IN THE PULPIT

"Good Night, Honey"

GLADYS TABER

We always think of Christmas as a time of snow and icicles hanging from the old well and snow over the valley. But I had a friend who was newly married and went to live in the tropics. She felt sorry for herself as Christmas drew near. She wept. And then her husband brought in some tropical flowers, to decorate the house, he said. And it came to her suddenly that Christmas was not a place, nor was it weather, it was a state of mind. After all, she thought, Christ was not born in the North, he was born in a stable in Bethlehem. And so she got a small palm tree and put flowers on the flat leaves, and was gay and merry. It was, she said, one of the best Christmases ever, although they afterward moved back to New England where the snow fell and the pine trees were silvered.

It is certainly true that Christmas is only seasonal in the heart. The snow may be clean and deep outside, or you may be in a dingy city apartment or you may be in a steaming tropical country. But it is still Christmas. Whether you serve the plump crispy turkey, or something exotic wrapped in pandanus leaves, the feeling of Christmas is there. It is in the mind and in the heart. The faith we have in the good rises like a tide and wherever we are, we feel it. Christmas graces any board and gives a new lift to our life, and as we hear once more the familiar carols, we thank God for the birth of His son. "O little town of Bethlehem, how still we see thee lie—Above thy dark and dreamless streets the silent stars go by."

As always when the old house creaks into quiet, I snuff the Christmas candles, and check to be sure nobody has left a turkey bone where the Irish could get it. The colored ribbons and tissues are swept up, the fire has died down, and I let the cockers and Irish out for a last run in the new-fallen snow. They take nips of it, roll in it.

And now, as always, I have a special reunion with my Honey, a golden cocker who died a time ago. I hear her paws softly padding beside me as I put the house to bed. I can see her golden feather of tail wagging happily. Some might say this is foolish for she was, after all, only a dog, and she is dead. But the fourteen years of love and loyalty she gave me are very much alive as I say "Good night, Honey."

The house talks, as old houses do. A beam settles. A chair rocks. A floor creaks with unseen footsteps. I like this, for it reminds me of all the lives that have been lived under this roof, and I feel their friendly presence as I poke the embers. Christmas is over. It is time to burn the wrappings, write the thank-you notes, return the calls, set the house in order for the New Year. It is also time to consider where our lives are bound, what purpose steadies our course. How much have we helped our fellow men this year, and what good have we accomplished? Has the world been better because we were in it? If Christmas means anything, it means good will to all. I doubt many of us truly live up to that, but we can try again.

As I let the dogs back in, I smell the snow. The walk is silver, the picket fence wears pointed caps. Night herself is luminous with the falling snow. A flurry comes in with the dogs and melts on the wide floor boards. No two snowflakes,

I am told, are exactly alike and this is a mystery. Now the intricate shapes are gone, and only a spot of water remains. It is not very practical to stand in the open door at midnight and let the snow blow in. But it has been my habit for years to close Christmas Day just so, sending my blessing out to all the people in the world, those I know well and love greatly, and those I shall never see. And as I close the door, I repeat again my Christmas blessing.

"God rest you merry, gentlemen."

from STILLMEADOW SAMPLER

Mrs. Donovan

JAMES HERRIOT

*I*nspector Halliday of the RSPCA rang me. "Mr. Herriot," he said, "I'd like you to come and see an animal with me. A cruelty case."

"Right, what is it?"

"A dog, and it's pretty grim. A dreadful case of neglect." He gave me the name of a row of old brick cottages down by the river and said he'd meet me there.

Halliday was waiting for me, smart and business-like in his dark uniform, as I pulled up in the back lane behind the houses.

"He's in here," he said, and led the way towards one of the doors in the long, crumbling wall. A few curious people were hanging around and with a feeling of inevitability I recognised a gnome-like brown face. Trust Mrs. Donovan, I thought, to be among those present at a time like this.

Halliday went over to a ramshackle wooden shed with peeling paint and a rusted corrugated iron roof. He produced a key, unlocked the padlock and dragged the door partly open. There was no window and it wasn't easy to identify the jumble inside: broken gardening tools, an ancient mangle, rows of flower pots and partly used paint tins. And right at the back, a dog sitting quietly.

I didn't notice him immediately because of the gloom and

because the smell in the shed started me coughing, but as I drew closer I saw that he was a big animal, sitting very upright, his collar secured by a chain to a ring in the wall. I had seen some thin dogs but this advanced emaciation reminded me of my text books on anatomy; nowhere else did the bones of pelvis, face and rib cage stand out with such horrifying clarity. A deep, smoothed-out hollow in the earth floor showed where he had lain, moved about, in fact lived for a very long time.

The sight of the animal had a stupefying effect on me; I only half took in the rest of the scene—the filthy shreds of sacking scattered nearby, the bowl of scummy water.

"Look at his back end," Halliday muttered.

I carefully raised the dog from his sitting position and realised that the stench in the place was not entirely due to the piles of excrement. The hindquarters were a welter of pressure sores which had turned gangrenous, and strips of sloughing tissue hung down from them. There were similar sores along the sternum and ribs. The coat, which seemed to be a dull yellow, was matted and caked with dirt.

The Inspector spoke again. "I don't think he's ever been out of here. He's only a young dog—about a year old—but I understand he's been in this shed since he was an eight-week-old pup. Somebody out in the lane heard a whimper or he'd never have been found."

I felt a tightening of the throat and a sudden nausea which wasn't due to the smell. It was the thought of this patient animal sitting starved and forgotten in the darkness and filth for a year. I looked again at the dog and saw in his eyes only a calm trust.

"Well, Inspector, I hope you're going to throw the book at whoever's responsible," I said.

Halliday grunted. "Oh, there won't be much done. They'll

fine him and stop him keeping an animal in the future but nothing more than that."

"I see." I reached out and stroked the dog's head and he immediately responded by resting a paw on my wrist. There was a pathetic dignity about the way he held himself erect, the calm eyes regarding me, friendly and unafraid. "Well, you'll let me know if you want me in court."

"Of course, and thank you for coming along." Halliday hesitated for a moment. "And now I expect you'll want to put this poor thing out of his misery right away."

I continued to run my hand over the head and ears while I thought for a moment. "Yes . . . yes, I suppose so. We'd never find a home for him in this state. It's the kindest thing to do. Anyway, push the door wide open will you so that I can get a proper look at him."

In the improved light I examined him more thoroughly. Perfect teeth, well-proportioned limbs with a fringe of yellow hair. I put my stethoscope on his chest and as I listened to the slow, strong thudding of the heart the dog again put his paw on my hand.

I turned to Halliday. "You know, Inspector, inside this bag of bones there's a lovely healthy Golden Retriever. I wish there was some way of letting him out."

As I spoke I noticed there was more than one figure in the door opening. A pair of black pebble eyes were peering intently at the big dog from behind the Inspector's broad back. The other spectators had remained in the lane but Mrs. Donovan's curiosity had been too much for her. I continued conversationally as though I hadn't seen her.

"You know, what this dog needs first of all is a good shampoo to clean up his matted coat."

"Huh?" said Halliday.

"Yes. And then he wants a long course of some really strong condition powders."

"What's that?" The Inspector looked startled.

"There's no doubt about it," I said. "It's the only hope for him, but where are you going to find such things? Really powerful enough, I mean." I sighed and straightened up. "Ah well, I suppose there's nothing else for it. I'd better put him to sleep right away. I'll get the things from my car."

When I got back to the shed Mrs. Donovan was already inside examining the dog despite the feeble remonstrances of the big man.

"Look!" she said excitedly, pointing to a name roughly scratched on the collar. "His name's Roy."

She stood silent for a few moments, obviously in the grip of a deep emotion, then she burst out.

"Can I have 'im? I can make him better, I know I can. Please, please let me have 'im!"

Halliday looked at her in bewilderment, then he said: "Excuse me, Madam," and drew me to one side.

"Mr. Herriot," he whispered. "I don't know what's going on here, but I can't just pass over an animal in this condition to anybody who has a casual whim. The poor beggar's had one bad break already—I think it's enough. This woman doesn't look a suitable person . . . "

I held up a hand. "Believe me, Inspector, you've nothing to worry about. She's a funny old stick but she's been sent from heaven today. If anybody in Darrowby can give this dog a new life it's her."

"All right, you seem very sure." Halliday looked at me for a second or two then turned and walked over to the eager little figure by the shed.

• • •

I had never before been deliberately on the lookout for Mrs. Donovan: she had just cropped up wherever I happened to be, but now I scanned the streets of Darrowby anxiously day by day without sighting her. Maybe I should have called round to see how she was getting on with that dog. Certainly I had trimmed off the necrotic tissue and dressed the sores before she took him away, but perhaps he needed something more than that. And yet at the time I had felt a strong conviction that the main thing was to get him out of there and clean him and feed him and nature would do the rest. And I had a lot of faith in Mrs. Donovan—far more than she had in me—when it came to animal doctoring; it was hard to believe I'd been completely wrong.

It must have been nearly three weeks and I was on the point of calling at her home when I noticed her stumping briskly along the far side of the market-place, peering closely into every shop window exactly as before. The only difference was that she had a big yellow dog on the end of the lead.

I turned the wheel and sent my car bumping over the cobbles till I was abreast of her. When she saw me getting out she stopped and smiled impishly, but she didn't speak as I bent over Roy and examined him. He was still a skinny dog but he looked bright and happy, his wounds were healthy and granulating and there was not a speck of dirt in his coat or on his skin. I knew then what Mrs. Donovan had been doing all this time; she had been washing and combing and teasing at that filthy tangle till she had finally conquered it.

As I straightened up she seized my wrist in a grip of surprising strength and looked up into my eyes.

"Now Mr. Herriot," she said, "haven't I made a difference to this dog!"

"You've done wonders, Mrs. Donovan," I said. "And you've

been at him with that marvellous shampoo of yours, haven't you?"

She giggled and walked away and from that day I saw the two of them frequently but at a distance and something like two months went by before I had a chance to talk to her again. She was passing by the surgery as I was coming down the steps and again she grabbed my wrist.

"Mr. Herriot," she said, just as she had done before, "haven't I made a difference to this dog!"

I looked down at Roy with something akin to awe. He had grown and filled out and his coat, no longer yellow but a rich gold, lay in luxuriant shining swathes over the well-fleshed ribs and back. A new, brightly studded collar glittered on his neck and his tail, beautifully fringed, fanned the air gently. He was now a Golden Retriever in full magnificence. As I stared at him he reared up, plunked his fore paws on my chest and looked into my face, and in his eyes I read plainly the same calm affection and trust I had seen back in that black, noisome shed.

"Mrs. Donovan," I said softly, "he's the most beautiful dog in Yorkshire."

I suppose you could say that that was the start of Roy's second life. And as the years passed I often pondered on the beneficent providence which had decreed that an animal which had spent his first twelve months abandoned and unwanted, staring uncomprehendingly into that unchanging, stinking darkness, should be whisked in a moment into an existence of light and movement and love. Because I don't think any dog had it quite so good as Roy from then on.

His diet changed dramatically from odd bread crusts to best stewing steak and biscuit, meaty bones and a bowl of warm milk every evening. And he never missed a thing. Garden fêtes, school sports, evictions, gymkhanas—he'd be there. I was pleased to note that as time went on Mrs. Donovan seemed to be clocking up an even greater daily mileage. Her expenditure on shoe leather must have been phenomenal, but of course it was absolute pie for Roy—a busy round in the morning, home for a meal, then straight out again; it was all go.

Mrs. Donovan, too, had her reward; she had a faithful companion by her side every hour of the day and night. But there was more to it than that; she had always had the compulsion to help and heal animals and the salvation of Roy was the high point of her life—a blazing triumph which never dimmed.

I know the memory of it was always fresh because many years later I was sitting on the sidelines at a cricket match and I saw the two of them; the old lady glancing keenly around her, Roy gazing placidly out at the field of play, apparently enjoying every ball. At the end of the match I watched them move away with the dispersing crowd; Roy would have been about twelve then and heaven only knows how old Mrs. Donovan must have been, but the big golden animal was trotting along effortlessly and his mistress, a little more bent perhaps and her head rather nearer the ground, was going very well.

When she saw me she came over and I felt the familiar tight grip on my wrist.

"Mr. Herriot," she said, and in the dark probing eyes the pride was still as warm, the triumph still as bursting new as if it had all happened yesterday.

"Mr. Herriot, haven't I made a difference to this dog!"

from JAMES HERRIOT'S DOG STORIES

GENTLE TEACHERS

"But the greatest gift these
friends will share is knowing what
is in the other's heart."

CHRISTINE DAVIS

Whoever called an animal "dumb" never really knew one. If we pay attention, there's a lot we can learn from our best friends about the more important things in life. Such as accepting our weaknesses and forgiving us when we give in to them . . . how to keep going in spite of obstacles and handicaps . . . how to face our fears and get the better of them . . . how to appreciate the little blessings in life . . . and how to laugh at ourselves when we do something foolish.

Perhaps the most important lesson we can learn from our animal friends is to get closer to God. They seem to be born knowing how to do that, and they're only too happy to show us how.

Do You Remember Me?

C. W. GUSEWELLE

How much do animals know? How much do they remember?

With golden eyes as cool as ice he stared out through the wire of his kennel at the stranger coming toward him.

For his first 15 months of life he'd had a regular home—a yard, his own food dish, a park for exercise, a rug indoors for inclement nights. Then he'd had to be boarded out, kenneled in a place with dozens of other dogs, a clamorous company, and given over to the companionship of another man.

What sense did he make of that? None, most likely. One morning he was loaded in the car, as so many happy times before. And after traveling awhile he was taken out and led past other boarders raging at their wires, and locked in any empty pen. And the car and the man went unexplainably away.

After that the other man, the different one, came regularly. In the autumn they would spend a day or two days together looking for quail and pheasants. Then he would go back to the pen. Autumn turned to bitter winter. There was straw in his box, and maybe he slept warm, or maybe not. Certainly there was no rug on a heated floor. A year he spent there, and that was nearly half his life so far—long enough you would think he might have forgotten all that went before.

Now this stranger was walking toward his pen and, for a fact, in those flat, golden eyes there was not a sign of recognition.

I put down a hand. A nose was thrust cautiously toward it. There was a moment's uncertainty. Then his face turned up— looked directly into mine. The yellow eyes were no longer cool, detached. There was familiarity in them. They were full of things recalled.

His time away is finished now. But what can he possibly understand of this strange experience? Nothing, I suppose, although surely he will remember it. Any creature that remembers home must also remember exile. Nor is he apt ever to forget that other man whose visits and excursions gave purpose to those weeks.

What he does seem to understand is that the exile is over—not just interrupted but really finished. Perfectly unperturbed, he sleeps again on his rug or on his chair, as if he'd never left them. When called to ride in the car he goes gladly, expecting only good, never imagining he might again be left.

My explanation of all of this would be lost on him, and anyway he does not seem to require one. Intuition tells him all he needs to know. He's home. He sleeps warm. And that's how it will always be. Some men learn about forgiveness by studying the lives of saints. And some of us keep dogs.

from THE RUFUS CHRONICLE

Loyalty Is Serious Business

GLADYS TABER

I have never been able to understand the cat versus dog controversy. Cats are themselves, dogs are themselves. That is all there is to it. A well-furnished home has both. From a dog you get the passionate dependence, from a cat you get a sense that you must be worthy or the cat would simply move away. A cat is loyal, and has plenty of affection but it is on the basis that she or he grants it to you as a favor, and you must be grateful. A dog is wholly dependent, a cat wholly independent.

An example of the difference is that when I used to have to go away briefly, the dogs met me with wags and wild barks and carryings on. The cats spoke to me only in cold tones, implying that I was not worth bothering with. I went away. The Siamese went further, and cursed roundly in Siamese. The warm welcome of the cockers and Irish was fine, but the bitter remarks of the cats was fine too. In the end, they always forgave me for deserting them for a night and with great condescension acquired the warmest spot on my bed. After a few hours, the Siamese would give me a few licks with a sandpapery tongue. There was no mistake, she was forgiving me.

The Manx, Tigger, simply gave me a chilly look and vanished for the rest of the day. Let me worry where HE was, he had worried as to where I was. Around suppertime, he would mellow, and come in with a mouse. And when I screamed and took it away and put it outside, he sat down on the hearth and washed himself elaborately, saying plainly, Well, there it is, a man does his best, and what thanks does he get?

Esmé, the Siamese, had a fine sense of humor. She enjoyed sitting at the top of the stairs behind the stair rail. When an unwary cocker would come up, she shot out a sudden arm and slapped him soundly, her expression like that of the legendary Cheshire cat. She also liked to get inside a paper bag and suddenly an animated paper bag would fly around the room, most disconcerting to both cockers and Irish. She would pounce on me suddenly from the bookshelves and loved it when I dropped an armload of clean clothes.

The love affair between Esmé and Tigger was touching. He was by nature a sober, industrious cat who worked hard at his mouse business. Esmé was a femme fatale and also flighty. They would sleep with their paws around each other's neck, Tigger having done a hard night's work in the cellar. Suddenly Esmé, bored with peace, would turn on him and growl fiercely, pulling bitefuls of black fur from his neck. If he ignored this (just wanting to rest his feet and look at TV, as it were) she would pounce, attack, retreat, roll on the floor, address him plaintively. You don't give a fig for me, she would say in her firm Siamese voice. Was it for this I became your companion? The best years of my life, etc., etc. He would shrug and eye her with his big topaz eyes. I bring home the mice, he would indicate.

Mice never meant anything in her life. He would lug in a good one and lay it tenderly at her paws, and she would flip it over idly and then turn her back. She never even thanked him.

But when he died, she never recovered. She sat upstairs in

the bathroom for a week. She ate almost nothing. She took her widow's weeds seriously. In time, she came back downstairs for chicken or spinach, but she was never gay again.

She did, however, condescend to catch one very small mouse in the barn and carry it delicately to the house and into my bedroom. She laid it on my bed and switched away, as if to assure me she could also be a mouser, but her heart was not in it.

We felt she needed another companion, and this proved to be disastrous. We brought home a blue-point Siamese named Moonlight, a nice conventional cat (the only Siamese I ever knew with this temperament). Esmé nearly killed him. We introduced them gently, with a screen door between them, we followed all the rules. But the first time she could reach him, the whole air was full of silvery fur and Moonlight fled screaming. We spent some weeks shutting doors and finally shutting Moonlight in a dog carrying-crate for protection. But Esmé would utter such jungle sounds as would do credit to a tiger at the kill and would fling herself at the crate. If we had any idea she would cotton to an interloper, we were put in our place. So when Moonlight developed an inferiority complex and shook most of the time, we had to give it up. He wasn't Tigger, and we had to realize that she would have none of him.

Whenever friends say they don't care for cats, because cats have no feeling and no personality, I think of Esmé. She had both to give away.

from STILLMEADOW SAMPLER

Three Little Kittens

PHYLLIS HOBE

In my rural area I often see barn cats hunting in the fields. In exchange for keeping the rodent population down they get food and shelter from farmers, but they aren't comfortable with people. If they wander onto my property, they run off as soon as they see me.

One morning, however, I found a cat curled up beneath the shrubs in front of my house. It was pregnant, a pretty little gray cat with black stripes. I brought out some food, which the cat gobbled up. She let me pet her and rubbed against me, purring. This was no barn cat. It was a family pet.

I called everyone in my neighborhood, but no one reported a missing cat. I tried the local police, the animal shelter, several veterinarians—with no success. It seemed probable she had been abandoned by her owners. It was also obvious that she was going to deliver her kittens very soon.

What was I to do? I couldn't bring her into my home because she might be diseased. But it was October, and though the days were warm, the nights were cold. At sunset she let me pick her up and I took her into my garage. She curled up on a pile of old towels and at that moment she went into labor.

For the next few hours I watched in awe as the cat delivered three kittens. From what I could see they were not only alive, but vigorous. "As soon as you can, start picking them up and petting them," my veterinarian said when I called him. "That way, when you want to find homes for them they'll be ready to live with people."

Find homes for three kittens? I hadn't thought of that. I called the animal shelter, but I was told if I brought them in they would have to be put to sleep immediately. "It's the way it is," the woman told me. "The newborns and mother might have diseases our other animals could catch." There was a sadness in her voice. "If you can keep them for six weeks, when they finish nursing we can take them in then."

Six weeks, I thought. *But maybe I can find them homes before that.*

My house isn't large and I already had two cats and one dog, so I carried the mother and her kittens down to the basement and piled newspapers and old towels in a box for a nesting place. Of course, my other animals were curious, and it took some athletic maneuvering to get past them every time I used the basement door.

"Lord, I've got six weeks," I prayed. "I need all the help you can give me." I called everyone I knew and passed the word. I ran an ad in the local paper. I even told people I didn't know well and asked them to tell their friends. I kept getting the same response: People who loved cats already had one or more. *Surely,* I told myself, *someone will come forward.*

No one did. As the weeks passed I felt uneasy. Was God going to abandon the animals just the way some human had? I couldn't believe that. But the kittens—two females and a male—were getting bigger, learning how to jump and climb, and I couldn't keep them in the basement much longer. My veterinarian examined them and gave them rabies shots, so I knew they were healthy.

But when I called the animal shelter they had bad news for me. They were overwhelmed with kittens; they couldn't promise to keep them for long. *I can't let them be put to sleep.*

On the last day of the sixth week I reminded God that we had come to our deadline yet nothing was happening. And then it hit me: I had given God an ultimatum. I had more or less told him I would have faith in him for six weeks and no more.

I was so ashamed. "Forgive me, Lord," I prayed. "I know you will help me find homes for these little ones. However long it takes, I'll look after them."

A sense of peace came over me. For the first time I allowed the kittens and their mother to follow me upstairs. I trusted my very friendly dog and cats to accept them, and after a bit of curious sniffing they did.

When the kittens were eight weeks old a friend of a friend called and asked if she could see them. When she did, she fell in love with them and took one of the females home with her. Two days later I had a call from a young couple whose cat had died a month earlier. "We miss him so much," the woman said. They took the rambunctious young male with them. By the next week the third kitten went home with the young man who delivers my fuel oil.

That left the mother cat, whom I decided to keep. Like my animals, she wasn't young and spent most of her time sleeping. But then I had a call from a friend's neighbor. "I'm getting on in years and so is my cat," the woman told me. "We need some company but neither of us can keep up with a kitten. I was wondering if you would let me have the mother."

These events happened three years ago, and all four cats are doing well. As for me, I learned a valuable lesson. Now when I need God's help I simply ask, knowing he will come to my aid. And I don't give him a deadline.

We Called Him Romeo

JACQUELINE DAMIAN

Out of all of Meeny's kittens, there was one that I loved the most: Romeo, who was born, along with his sister, Juliet, when I was six or seven. I begged and begged to keep him. Meeny was the family cat, dubbed Beanhead—Bean, for short—by my brother as soon as Mike was old enough to talk. But I wanted a cat of my own, one who was all mine, and I wanted one so badly that finally my parents said Romeo could stay.

He was not what you would call a handsome cat. In fact, he was actually somewhat homely. Buff pink and off-white, he grew up to be a burly, big-headed tomcat sorely lacking the usual feline grace. I loved him all the more for that, reasoning that because he was less than beautiful no one else could possibly appreciate him the way I did. An unneutered male (we didn't know from neutering back in the fifties), Romeo roamed. Sometimes he stayed away for a couple of days, returning to gobble up large servings of Puss 'n' Boots cat food and laze around the house before setting off on further adventures. "Wherefore art thou Romeo?" took on new meaning for us.

Sometimes Romeo came home bloodied from catfights, in which he ultimately acquired notched ears and a scarred nose, like an aging pugilist. But I know he gave as good as he got, for

I witnessed more than a few of these feline conflicts in or near our yard.

He ranged widely, and one time he came home covered from head to toe with soot. God knows where he had been; we didn't exactly live in an industrial district. We washed him in the kitchen sink with Breck shampoo. My brother and I cut up an old rain slicker to make four cat-size galoshes, which we fastened on Romeo's paws with fat rubber bands to keep him from scratching. My father held him down in the sink while my mother lathered and sprayed. I took a snapshot of this unusual event, which I still have.

For all of his street smarts Romeo was kind of awkward indoors, like a mountainman at a cotillion. For example, he never got used to the washing machine, which was in the kitchen, and skittered away in fear whenever my mother turned it on. Sometimes he careened smack into a wall in his haste to get away. By the time he got old he had lost most of his teeth, so instead of eating directly out of his dish he scooped up cat food with his right front paw and delivered it to his mouth like that. This never failed to amaze our visitors.

But he was my cat, and that was all that mattered. For years I carried Romeo's picture around in my wallet alongside snapshots of my parents and brother and my own First Communion photo. He slept on my bed every night (or every night he was home), curling up by my chest or in the cat-size crook formed by my bent knees when I slept on my side, where he would purr and purr. I was acutely aware of his comfort, and shimmied over to one side of the bed to give him enough room to stretch. He was a mellow, good-natured soul, not unlike my cat Charcoal today, and more tolerant of my friends than children have any right to expect of a cat. He let us dress him up in dolls' clothes and ride him around in my toy carriage.

I was heartbroken to get back from Girl Scout camp the summer I was eleven and find that Romeo was snubbing me. Unsure, perhaps, of who I was after my week-long absence, he refused to sleep with me for the first night I was home. Instead, he stationed himself in the doorway to my room all night, and no matter how many times I hauled him up on the bed beside me, he jumped back down and resumed his place by the door.

This was my first lesson in life from a cat. Romeo was informing me that one's actions have consequences.

from SASHA'S TAIL

Rupa and I— a Reason to Live

MAUREEN KEENAN-MASON

For being so small, fifty-four grams to be precise, Rupa radiated a large presence. Not many could ignore his uncanny ability to put our three household dogs into a down-stay when he walked from his cage to the window across the room. Rupa was a grey-cheek parakeet with a gutsy attitude toward life that glimmered like a crystal in the sun. In addition to his good looks, he had robust health until the seventh year of his life when he contracted avian tuberculosis. Rupa was given only a twenty percent chance to live, and to live for only a short span of time.

But Rupa didn't die. For four months he lived in our guestroom and fought the TB with everything his weakened forty-eight grams could muster. Rupa survived, but he lost most of his physical strength, forever. He was permanently deformed on his left side, often dragging his left leg, and he had to remain on medication indefinitely.

Rupa had numerous setbacks over the years, but his inner strength enabled him to struggle and succeed after each one. Rupa's will to live rang loud and clear—much louder than the ear-piercing jungle calls he used to make but no longer had the strength to scream.

It was Rupa's determination and his inner spirit that kept me going after years of my own pain, which eventually resulted in my having abdominal surgery. I was shuffling across the room, pitying myself, bemoaning my weakened state and the complications that had occurred after surgery. As I slowly passed by Rupa's cage, he chirped at me and lumbered over to the corner of his cage to visit me, dragging his left leg behind him. I looked at his slightly askew body as he struggled toward me, using all the strength he could muster just to say "hello." But I heard more than a greeting. I heard, "Never give up. Keep going. Don't look back, deal with it. Life is too short to let illness become your focus." They were indeed the words Rupa lived by. I don't think any card, well-wisher, or medication could have altered my perspective on health and healing more than Rupa did in that moment, as I watched him make his way to see me, taking longer and working harder to do it.

I still have pains from my surgery. When I begin to sadden because I am not "up to par," I see Rupa, dragging his left leg, using what strength he had with gusto, not dwelling on what used to be or might have been. And I do what he would do. I move forward with my life.

I have to rely on my memories of Rupa these days because he died several months ago. His spirit lives on inside of me. And I often wonder if that twinge in my belly is a result of my surgery, or an ache of longing for Rupa to return.

from ANIMALS AS TEACHERS & HEALERS

A Quiet Moment Together

ELEANOR SASS

---

*M*y new Dandie Dinmont terrier puppy Wally doesn't hesitate to let me know when he needs something. By a persistent bark or a cold-nose nudge, he tells me when he wants to eat, go outside or play.

Recently, I was sitting in my bedroom chair reading. Wally raised himself on his hind legs, his forepaws touching my lap. It wasn't his mealtime. He'd just come in from being outside. "Do you want to play?" I asked, reaching down for his yellow rubber ball. But when I threw it, Wally didn't run. Instead, he gave me another nudge with his nose.

"Do you want to come up here?" The answer seemed to be yes, because he attempted to jump. But he didn't make it. His legs were too short. So I lifted him up into my lap. After some turning and shifting, he settled down. When I heard him give a big sigh, a warm feeling of contentment enfolded me.

This is how God must feel, I thought, *when one of His children comes to Him, not with a need but simply wanting to be with Him, to have a quiet time in His lap.*

Minnie and the Rug

MARION BOND WEST

I was overjoyed when my husband Gene surprised me with a beautiful Persian area rug. For years I had admired them and wished that one day I could own one. It was perfect in front of our fireplace, picking up the dark green, beige and rose colors of our living room. As we stood admiring it, our cat Minnie stepped cautiously onto the plush rug and settled down in the center of a bouquet of pale pink roses.

"No!" I raised my voice. Our dear Minnie was surprised because she had unlimited access to every square inch of our house, and now I was trying to train her to respect this one bit of space. That night I got up to find Minnie back on the rug, sleeping on the roses once again. I scolded her, and she left reluctantly. Perhaps I *was* a bit overprotective, but for now, while the rug was brand-new, I didn't want to risk it getting soiled.

Then, very early one morning, I came downstairs and discovered that Minnie had positioned herself so that the tips of her front paws barely touched the fringe of the rug; the rest of her was safely not touching it at all! She looked at me very innocently and pitifully, purring, as if to say, "Surely you can't object to this!"

Well, I finally felt a little silly. Minnie just wanted a soft, comfortable spot to nap, and she seemed to enjoy those pink roses. After all, this wasn't a museum, but a living room, a room to live in. How could I turn away anyone, human or animal, seeking safety and warmth?

"It's okay, girl," I assured Minnie. She purred with her eyes closed and her paws barely touching the fringe of the new rug she so loved. I went back to bed . . . happily and drifted off to sleep thinking: *In any contest of wills between humans and felines, I know who usually wins.* Sleep came quickly.

"Help Me, Keesha!"

SUSAN CHERNAK McELROY

Keesha was my friend, my confidant, my angel and, ultimately, my teacher. I first began writing about Keesha and her powerful healing lessons while I was recuperating from radiation treatments for aggressive, metastatic neck cancer. Only thirty-seven when I was initially diagnosed with a malignant tumor in my mouth, my medical prognosis was poor. These tumors are usually found in old, cigar-smoking, heavy-drinking men. When they appear in young, clean-living women like me, they usually spread like a chemical fire. When the tumor advanced to my lymph nodes in 1988, my doctors didn't expect me to survive another two years.

Like so many of us who have lived the suburban, civilized life, I'd always been shielded from sickness and death (which I have since learned is no blessing), and I knew little about how to live with a serious illness, much less how to die from one. According to my doctors, there was no reason to believe that I wouldn't be dying, and soon.

A friend has a phrase for those who have either faced their own death and survived, or who have experienced the death of a loved one. He calls them "the Initiated." The words, "You have cancer," launched my initiation. A sickening riot of feelings cemented my new-found status as initiate: Terror, hysteria, retching fear—these words described me on my good days. Because no one in my family or circle of friends had ever faced a serious or terminal illness, they could offer no counsel aside from their own terror at watching a relatively young woman face a grim prognosis. Where was I to find examples of how to live what was left of my life? Where does an initiate go for help? Finding no answers among anyone I knew, I turned to the only hopeful memory I had: Keesha.

In 1981, Keesha had died of cancer. Her disease started exactly where mine had, in the mouth. Her symptoms were the same as mine, including problems with eating and swallowing. Keesha's treatments were the same, too: weeks of daily radiation. Keesha eventually died of her disease, but she lived with remarkable zest and exuberance until the end. Suddenly, years after her death, Keesha and I were together once again, this time in the spirit of similar circumstance, and I felt a renewed bond with her. In my memories of Keesha, I would find the help I was seeking.

During the year-long course of my surgeries, metastases, and treatments it was Keesha's example I chose to follow. When I was in the first stages of cancer what I valued most were my memories of Keesha's complete and graceful acceptance of every part of her illness and debilitation. One incident in particular had a profound impact on me, and even more so years later. Several weeks before her death, Keesha had become quite weak from her disease. The long daily strolls along the marsh near our home became shorter and slower as her cancer spread. In her healthiest days, Keesha's greatest joy had been to swim in the deep lagoons filled with cattails and marsh grass. But now, too frail to swim, she looked to the glossy, shallow pools of rain that peppered our streets. At every opportunity, Keesha would plop into a big puddle and splash and bark for as long as I'd let her. The look on her face during those times was the look of a hog in a wallow. On our last excursion together she was only days away from death, yet she was in bliss.

From a dog splashing in a rain puddle, I learned about choice. Regardless of how much time I had left, I could choose to celebrate whatever possibilities life had to offer me each moment. Or, I could curl up and die. We, the Initiated, can be possessed by a manic sense of urgency and dread unknown to most people. It is a curse and a blessing. The urgency keeps your priorities straight, but it can paralyze momentum and cripple one's best efforts with fear. The antidote to that fear is to practice joy in the moment. I learned that the choice between celebration or dread is mine. Keesha's lesson is still with me today and has changed how I am in the world. At joy, Keesha was a master.

Through Keesha's inspiration, I somehow kept my humor, most of my friends, and my activities while undergoing cancer treatment. It would be a kindly understatement to say I had been dragged kicking and whining through the previous three-plus decades of my life. Always believing that life owed me something, I would complain bitterly when I didn't get what I thought I deserved. Sarcasm and rebelliousness were my most characteristic coping tools, and fear about anything and everything was my prime motivator. By the time I was faced with cancer, I was a sick, scared little girl. I truly believe that Keesha and cancer matured and healed me.

from ANIMALS AS TEACHERS & HEALERS

The Mouser-Cat

ANNA MORETTI

Girls need women. Students need teachers. Apprentices need masters. Acorns need the shade and richness of the oak grove. A heart needs empathy. Everyone needs someone to shelter and protect them, to give them the courage to pursue their dreams, to not be afraid, to summon the will to *be* what they were meant to become.

Who would have guessed my teacher, my master, my mentor from girl to woman would be Mouser, my beloved Mouser-Cat?

I was a young girl when the Mouser came into my life; the Mouser, who would prove wise beyond her years, was then only a tiny kitten. Dad let the Mouser into my life on one condition: She would live in the barn to take care of the mice who came in to steal the horse's grain. But when I brought the tiny black-and-white kitten home from the shelter, my dad, with whom Mouser must have been sharing some of her wisdom already, said, "You can't put that little thing out in the barn. She'll freeze to death."

So we compromised: The kitten lived in my bedroom, and we called her "Mouser," nickname "The Mouser-Cat," to keep dad happy.

Mouser, I think, knew our great expectations for her and

became the most aggressive mousing cat ever known to humankind except . . . well . . . she seemed to think it was her duty to rid the world not of threats to the horse's grain, but to me.

Mouser, alas, had trouble distinguishing mice from dogs that came near me. It was dogs that she viciously chased from the house (even the ones who lived in it!), dogs she lay in ambush for in the front yard, howling dogs, screaming for their lives, she chased down the street with me running after her.

"You've got to do something about that cat," Mom warned me. "She's terrorizing the neighborhood."

But I didn't do anything about that cat because I *couldn't.* Mouser made it clear from the beginning that it was *me* who belonged to *her.* She was terribly possessive of me. I think, in her catlike wisdom, she understood my fears of the big, wide world. And protect me she did!

Raise your voice at me and she would raise hers at you. She was very serious about protecting what belonged to her—and if her voice couldn't convince you of her intent, her claws would.

When my car was stolen, along with my house keys, a locksmith was called to change the door locks to my apartment. I got an urgent call at work, "You're going to have to come down here after all, Ma'am," he said kindly. "Your cat won't let me in the apartment."

When Mouser wasn't protecting me, she was equally assertive meeting her own needs. Mouser, you see, got everything she wanted from me, her best friend, including two meals a day. Mouser seldom failed to remind me that meals were to be served every morning and every night; and when she did fail to remind me, I'd sneak off to work or off to sleep, hoping she would never remember—because Mouser could stand to lose a few pounds.

One night, I'd been in bed for a good half hour when a horrible cat cry at bedside awoke me. I snapped on the night lamp and leaned over the mattress. Mouser was sitting there, blinking up at me with that "You thought I'd forget again, didn't you?" expression while a can of Fancy Feast sat nestled on the carpet between her front paws. She'd carried it in from the kitchen.

But as determined as Mouser was at voicing her own opinion, she was equally affectionate—with me, that is, her possession. I would lie on the sofa, tap the center of my chest, and say, "Kiss? Kiss?"; and she would oblige me, leap onto my chest, press her forehead against my lips, and take as many kisses as a cat could stand. "The things some animals have to endure," she seemed to be saying, "just to get fed."

Mouser wasn't afraid of anything, even death. After thirteen years, the veterinarian told me what I'd feared most: He thought Mouser's kidneys and liver were cancerous. If exploratory surgery proved his worst suspicions, he asked me, "Should we let her go? Or should we bring her out of anesthesia to give us one more week, or one more day, or even one more moment, to say good-bye again?"

My answer caught in my throat. It was a question I couldn't even face. If Mouser left me, my heart would break. My life would never be the same without her. She had been my best friend since I was a young girl.

The night before her surgery, we were lying together on the cool kitchen floor. There was a dying light in her gaze that was fixed on the wall beyond me. She had lost so much weight she was merely a skeleton, and she hadn't eaten in days. I couldn't force one more pill down her throat. I wept with guilt when she fought me—as if she *wanted* to die and I wouldn't let her.

And I was weeping that night, lying on the floor with her,

asking her with anguish in the hope she would understand: "What should I do, Mouser? Do you want me to let you go?"

As we lay there, only my crying audible, a flash of light came into Mouser's eyes. She turned her head in my direction and met my gaze. For a long minute that I had wished would be an eternity, she looked at me, almost through me. My eyes filled with tears and hers with an unexplainable smile.

"What?" I begged her silently. "Do you have the answer?"

She was only a few inches from my face; she pressed her forehead to my lips and asked me for a kiss.

"Do what is best for me," I believe she said. "I can accept life better than you can; after all these long, full years, I can accept death as well. In the end, doing what's best for me will bring peace to both our lives."

In the dying light of her eyes I felt Mouser was telling me: do not be afraid. Of life, or death. Or anything in between.

So the next day I did what Mouser had asked for in her kiss.

The kiss good-bye.

"Yes," I told the doctor finally of my decision. "Let her go."

I grieved and cried for many weeks for Mouser, my best friend. And if there is a lesson to this grief, it would be this, I must tell you: It is not an intangible thing we are removing from our midst when we kill the millions of dogs and cats every year in animal shelters across the country. It isn't a single ID number or a solitary statistic that dies when the light in a single cat's eyes dies. When we kill a million dogs and cats, we're killing a million lives who could touch us and heal us and bring us a kind of joy and warmth and peace in ways our fellow humans cannot. We're robbing a million beings of a million rays of sunlight, a million memories, a million heartbeats, a million lights of life.

We're killing a million Mousers.

And it was Mouser, after all, who taught me: Boldness has more to offer than fear. Life has more to offer than death.

That shelter kitten is waiting for you. *Go.*

Night Visitor

JACKIE GEYER

For twenty-some years, we've had a feeding station for neighborhood raccoons. Around the mid-1980s one late evening, a very small, young female showed up by herself at our station. I was horrified to see she was terribly hurt. Her right hind leg was a bloody stump. I couldn't tell if she had been hit by a car, caught in a trap, or what, but she was an awful sight. She was limping on her remaining hind leg and was quite disheveled. The food was already gone. I put more out as she hobbled to hide under a bush. As I came inside, she came to the plate and was immediately ferociously attacked by the other raccoons. She retreated, and this became the pattern.

Each night she would show up later and later to avoid the other raccoons. I began waiting up for her to make sure she got food and water. She came, faithfully, each night, around 1 to 3, after all the others had gone. Her stump began to heal, and she learned to adjust her other hind leg to center her body and balance herself. I hadn't named the others, but I felt a very warm attachment to this horribly injured raccoon. She had become my special charge. I named her Chloé.

My desk is next to the patio doors at the back of the house, and sometimes late at night I'd hear a tap on the glass, and there would be Chloé, looking in at me. She became my buddy.

One evening she didn't show up, and I began to worry about her. Then, very late, I saw her struggling to get to the station. She was using her two front legs to drag her body down the slope to the patio. Something had happened to her only good hind leg. When I saw her, I began sobbing hysterically. The sight of such pain and suffering broke my heart. Here was this sweet little raccoon who already had one missing leg to deal with, and now this. It was so cruel and unfair, I just couldn't bear it. I thought maybe if I could find a way to catch her, perhaps my vet could do something for her.

I stared at her through my tears as she ate her food and sat there on the patio for a long, long while. Then, to my never-ending surprise, she slowly put her two front legs forward and hoisted her back end into the air and started walking on her front legs! She walked for several feet, rested, and did it again. I started bawling all over again, partly because of her plight, and partly because I was so touched by her ingenuity and strength. This wonderful little creature was trying desperately to overcome her misfortune, and she was doing it.

She got through that first winter just fine. Her injured hind leg healed again. In the spring, I panicked once again when she didn't show up for two weeks—and then she showed up at my patio door with three fuzzy babies in tow! I went nuts: Chloé was a first-time mother.

That was eight years ago. I'm happy to report that Chloé is still here. Several generations of her kits are now my "regulars." Still, I'll never forget that fantastic sight of her doing handstands and walking all over my patio. . . . When I am feeling sorry for myself, all I have to do is think of dear little Chloé and I snap out of it immediately. Chloé is a lesson in perseverance I'll cherish forever.

from ANIMALS AS TEACHERS & HEALERS

Stowaway

STUART REININGER

I huddled behind the canopy as the sailboat hurtled through the starless night. Rain rattled against the not-so-protective canvas. A trickle found its way past my slicker and down my back. I was tired, wet and cold. I glanced at my watch: 3:00 A.M. Another hour until my daughter, Karin, would come on deck so I could snatch a few moments of sleep.

This trip—to deliver a charter company's 35-foot sloop from New York to St. Thomas in the U.S. Virgin Islands—was not going well. I had planned it as a watch-and-learn excursion for Karin, but a seasoned sailor I had invited canceled at the last minute, leaving just the two of us to sail the boat. Karin was only 14 and inexperienced, but she thought she was an old salt. She nagged me for more responsibilities, like standing a night watch by herself. That would have made my life a lot easier, but whenever she was on duty I only dozed. I couldn't trust her to handle the boat alone, especially in this squally weather.

We were five days into a projected 10-day voyage, but still far from the halfway point. Head winds and foul weather had slowed us down. The *Taurus,* a luxury craft designed for sheltered waters, required constant attention to keep it on course in the open sea.

Battling to keep my eyes open, I heard a soft fluttering over the patter of rain, followed by a muted thump. I turned around, and there, unaccountably, was a bedraggled pigeon.

"Well, hello, Pidge. How'd you get way out here?" I reached my hand out in greeting. "Welcome aboard, pal. We don't have much, but we'll be glad to share it with you."

"Brrrrck." *Snap!*

"Ouch!" I quickly withdrew my bloodied hand. "Ungrateful wretch."

The waterlogged bird glared. Then, doing the pigeon equivalent of muttering under its breath, he tucked his beak under a wing, while keeping a beady eye warily focused on me.

"Wow! Look at the pigeon," Karin exclaimed when she emerged from the cabin for her watch.

"Watch out," I warned, flaunting my pecked hand. "He's armed and dangerous."

After making sure Karin was holding the boat on course, I headed below and drifted into a fitful sleep. I awoke at sunrise to find *Taurus* slicing through calmer seas. Karin looked confident at the helm. I glanced at the compass—right on course. Behind me the aft deck was deserted. Our unwelcome guest must have departed—but not before leaving a mess where he had perched.

"Have a nice nap, Dad?" Karin asked. With her wide grin and damp blond hair plastered to her forehead, she looked even younger than her 14 years. I knew she was fishing for a compliment. She *had* done a good job handling the boat. But if I let her know that, she would hassle me for more responsibility.

"Yeah," I said, gesturing aft. "Glad we got rid of that nuisance. I'll clean the mess up."

A grimace of disappointment clouded Karin's face, but her smile soon returned. It was the kind she flashed when she knew she had put one over on me. I turned to go below.

"Brrrrck!"

I spun around. Peeking out from under her arm was the bird, its beady black eyes fixed on me malevolently.

"What's he doing here?" I asked.

"He's friendly," Karin gushed. "He came right over to me. You guys just got off on the wrong wing. C'mon and make up with Pidge."

I edged toward them carefully.

"Brrrrck!" *Snap!*

"Ouch!"

That set the tone for Pidge's and my relationship—an armed truce with mutual hostility. After it became obvious the bird was not going to leave, Karin begged me to allow it to occupy the closet where we hung our foul-weather gear.

I reluctantly agreed, but while her relationship with Pidge blossomed, ours wilted. As both a captain and a parent I retreated into a bunker of gruff authority. On our seventh day out, I woke up from an uncomfortable catnap on deck. The seas were building and lowering clouds indicated we were headed for nasty weather. Suspecting a long stay at the helm, I went below to get my new set of Helly-Hansen foul-weather gear.

I pulled my gear out and . . . *yuck!* They were splotched with a gooey yellow-green mess.

"My Hellys!" I hollered. "Look what that bird's done to my Hellys."

Furious, I rushed on deck and grabbed Pidge.

"Dad!" Karin yelled in alarm.

"This bird's got to go," I cried. "I've had it."

In a rage I tossed the pigeon into the air. I expected him to fly—probably right back to Karin. But he didn't. Screeching, he fluttered into the water and disappeared in our wake.

I looked in astonishment. *What have I done?*

Karin grew hysterical. "Why did you do that?" she cried. "You killed him!"

"I'm sorry," I mumbled. "I thought he would fly. I don't know why he didn't. He's a *bird,* for heaven's sake."

"We have to go back and get him," Karin yelled.

I was certain we would never find Pidge, yet I knew my relationship with my daughter would be destroyed if I didn't try.

We were at least two miles from where Pidge had disappeared by the time we struck the sails and started back under the engine's power. There was no telling how far we had drifted off our return course line. The wind and seas continued to increase, and spray cut visibility down even more. It would be a miracle if we were to return to the bird's location, much less find him.

After a half hour and no sign of him, I turned the boat back on course.

"It's no use, sweetheart. He's gone. We have to get going."

"Just a few minutes more," Karin pleaded.

After five minutes of futile slogging into the seas, I got back on course. Karin's face was etched with agony, and tears streamed from her eyes. She avoided looking at me. *God,* I wondered, *how can I make this up to her?* I looked out to sea as my eyes blurred with tears.

And there, about 50 yards off our port bow, was Pidge.

"I knew you'd find him, Dad! Thank you. Thank you," Karin cried as she hugged me.

Pidge swam with one wing flopping uselessly at his side, obviously injured. Then suddenly, just a few feet from *Taurus,* Pidge gave out. One moment he was alive, the next, a limp gray rag in the water.

"I'm sorry, Honey," I said. "He's gone."

Her voice rose. "We have to get him."

"We can't. There's no way. I can't leave the wheel—"

"I'll take the wheel," she said. "You use the wash bucket to scoop him up."

But that meant Karin would have to handle the boat while I hung over the edge of the deck. It would be a complex maneuver. If I fell overboard while trying to retrieve the bird, there was no way Karin would be able to get me back on board. It wasn't worth it. The bird was dead anyway.

I started to tell her this, then saw the look in her eyes. It went beyond retrieving a dead bird. It had to do with the trust and faith she had given me all her life. It was time for me to do the same for her.

"Okay," I said. I grabbed the bucket and went forward. Lying on my stomach, I hooked my foot on a deck stanchion and prayed I wouldn't fall. I heard the engine slip in and out of gear as Karin skillfully worked the boat toward Pidge. There he was—limp and lifeless—rising on a swell. I swung the bucket out. Just then the boat lurched and I began to slide overboard. I grabbed a stanchion and levered myself back on deck with one hand. The other held the bucket. In it was Pidge. I reached inside.

"Brrrrck." *Snap!*

Pidge reassumed his perch next to Karin and continued to eye me malevolently. It was obvious he wasn't going to change his mind about me, but I had changed my mind about Karin. Over supper that night I told her, "You did a fine job handling the boat today. As a matter of fact, you've turned into a darn good sailor. It's great to have you aboard."

She looked at me, her eyes glistening. I saw they were no longer the eyes of a child. Something in them made me want to continue. "I know I've always been stern with you, but I did it because I wanted to be a good father—to try to bring out your best. From now on I'm going to value you for what you are. I'm proud of you, and I love you."

Karin reached across the table to hold my hand. "Thank you, Dad. I love you too."

For the rest of the voyage Karin and I were partners. I trusted her on her watch, and she became proficient in seamanship and navigation. It took Pidge three days to recover, but he still glared and squawked whenever I appeared on deck.

When the mountains of St. Thomas finally came in sight, Pidge cooed at Karin, gave me the evil eye once more and flew off. I wasn't sorry to see him go, yet I was philosophic about his passage with us. Sometimes it takes a nasty bird to teach an ornery father to put love first.

MAKING A DIFFERENCE

"*A friend loves at all times.*"

PROVERBS 17:17, NIV

The love of a best friend can change our lives. Even though an animal accepts us the way we are, we can't help but try to be a little better. We become more responsible, not only for the animal, but for ourselves. We're more considerate of someone else's feelings and needs. We become stronger when we realize how much our friend depends upon us. And as we are trusted, we become more trusting. We're not afraid to be gentle, patient and understanding because we know that a best friend will never hurt us.

Most important of all, we discover what a blessing it is to open up our hearts and let a friend come in to stay.

A Friend of Van's

VAN VARNER

$\mathcal{M}$y name is Shep. I am a Belgian shepherd, expected to herd sheep, but in the year and a half of my life I haven't seen any. You see, I've had trouble finding a home. First there was Heidi, who turned me over to a couple in New York City, but when the woman had a baby, I went to Betty Kelly to await adoption. *Why didn't they want to keep me?* I was nervous when I was told a man was coming to look at me. *Suppose I didn't measure up? Suppose I didn't like him?* And then Van arrived and, in an instant, none of the worries mattered. I bounded to him and he took me in his arms and I knew that I was his.

So another New York apartment. Very cozy. We got right into a routine: Up at five, he fixes my breakfast at the same time as he does his, then forty-five minutes in Central Park where he unleashes me, but I keep an eye on him as I scurry around. There are more walks during the day, but outside the dog run, the rest are on the leash. I've heard from country and even suburban dogs visiting the park that I was lucky to have so much freedom. I don't know, but who cares? I am with him.

Van hasn't had a dog since his pointer, Clay. Ten years. Imagine going so long. But I have inherited Clay's leash and bowl and have tried in every way to be a worthy replacement.

Sometimes I feel I am better, since I do not shed the way he did and I have a more beautiful tail. Yesterday Van took my head in his hands and spoke to me.

"You know, Shep," he said, "God's wisdom is phenomenal. I don't know why He formed this alliance between man and dogs, but I am awfully glad He did. I've been lonely. I've missed a wagging tail when I come home and the regimen you bring to my life. You and I are partners, yes?"

I gave him a big, fat lick.

No More Ghosts

GARY SHIEBLER

When I was a boy, I was convinced that a ghost lived in my bedroom closet. My parents had renovated the attic of our brown-shingled Dutch Colonial and turned it into two bedrooms—one for me and one for my younger brother. My brother's room was on the sunny south side of the house. It was a simple, boxy room with a couple windows and a small closet. My bedroom, on the north side, had spooky nooks, landings, and crawl spaces, sharp-angled ceilings that dipped to darkened corners, two tiny windows, and this massive closet. Almost every night before I went to sleep, the closet door would have to be closed.

On some brave nights, I would decide to leave the door open a crack. I would brazenly turn off the light, pull the covers up, and close my eyes.

I'd call to my brother in the next room, "Glenn?"

No answer. He always fell asleep before I did.

Then a rogue creak or mysterious thump would spring my eyes open and set my pulse racing. I would peek over the covers and watch the door like a hawk. The hall light would begin to play tricks with my wide eyes and tender imagination. The small crack of pitch black would begin to grow. The gold doorknob would slowly begin to turn and the tips of ghoulish fingers would appear, curling around the door frame.

"Daaadd! Come close the closet door!" I'd yell.

My dad would bound up the stairs, three steps at a time, and close the door for me. He would assure me that the ghost was not strong enough to open the door by himself. I don't think he ever tried to convince me the ghost wasn't there. He'd just always come to the rescue.

One Tuesday morning when I was three years old, a very thin, baked-potato-brown dog appeared outside our front door.

"I opened the door and he was just standing there," my mother remembers. "He was an absolute mess. I called your father at work and he immediately came home and took him up to Dr. Barry's. It turned out that he had one of the worst cases of mange he had ever seen. Dr. Barry didn't think he was going to make it. 'I'll try my best to save him,' he told me. 'But it's very serious.' In those days, the only way they treated such severe cases of mange was with arsenic.

"It was a miracle that he recovered," she recalled. "Slowly he regained his strength. And all of those bare patches of skin and brown mats of fur were soon replaced with as glorious an orange coat as I had ever seen."

We named him Rusty.

He would become the dog against which I would measure all others.

To this day, my mom says there will never be another dog like him. And though my memories of him are fuzzy and gilded by a simpler and more innocent time, an imprint on my heart says it is so.

With the passing of years, I have forgotten many of the details about Rusty. Most have dissolved into myth or are bound by stories shared at dinner tables and in holiday living rooms.

I look at old photographs.

I see a dog sitting beside me on a braided rug in front of a small Christmas tree.

I want to remember the touch of his fur.

I see a young boy sitting proudly on a blue bicycle with a dog standing beside him.

I want to remember the sound of his bark.

I see two brothers hugging a dog on a front lawn.

I want to remember.

But I can't.

It is too long ago.

A shepherd/collie mix, Rusty was as stately, handsome, and heroic as any dog I have ever known. His rich coat was indeed golden orange, except for the fantastic white blaze that ran down his broad and sturdy chest and the splash of white at the tip of his magnificent tail. He was my protector, my friend, my confidant, my hero. He was fiercely loyal and used to do battle with any dog that crossed the line of our property. He was serious and very task-oriented but never turned down an offer for a good wrestle on our front lawn.

He never got sick. Occasionally he would come home a bit banged up after a fight with his neighborhood rival, a street-tough little mutt named Frankie. But he always recovered quickly, and after a few days' rest he would be back outside making sure our yard was a safe place for my brother and me to have a catch.

Mom swears he never had a flea in his life.

He didn't appreciate being asked to do dog tricks. Every now and then he would begrudgingly shake your hand if you pestered him long enough.

Kisses?

Never.

My dad did dress him up once as the disguised wolf from Little Red Riding Hood. He valiantly obliged for one snapshot. I never told him it made the local paper.

He loved to chase cars. After one particular close call, I screamed and yelled and begged him to stop. I told him I didn't want to see him die. I was eight years old. He never did it again.

He would regularly disappear, sometimes for as long as three days. Mom would worry and fret. Dad would say he was just visiting his girlfriend. Then out of the blue he would show up at the bus stop, greet us with a smile and a wag or two, then escort us home. We never did find out where he went.

Once, he broke up a fight between me and the neighborhood bully. He was the big brother I never had, the childhood angel who watched over me at all times. He was truly a gift from God.

So on those nights when Dad would come up and close the closet door, I would always ask him to do one more thing—to call Rusty upstairs to stay with me. He would yell, "Rusty! Come here, boy!" Soon, I would hear his generous paws loping up the stairs. He would greet us with a smile and a wag or two and then dutifully jump up on the end of my bed, heave a hefty sigh, and fall asleep. And if the ceilings started playing tricks on me, or if doorknobs started to turn or curtains became ghostly, all I had to do was reach out with my toes and feel the warmth of Rusty's back, and I would know an angel was nearby.

A few weeks after Rusty died, my brother dreamed that Rusty flew in his bedroom window and sat on the end of his bed. My brother sat up and, to his amazement, Rusty started talking to him. They talked for a long time, about all the good times he had with our family. Then he said it was time for him to go. He flew out the window into the night.

Just like angels do.

from A SEARCH FOR THE PERFECT DOG

Earthquake!

KRISTIN VON KREISLER

One of the best parts of being a writer is that I can work in my office all day surrounded by my pets. Tigger, my tabby kitty, drapes herself across the Morris chair and makes occasional tiny squeaks that sound like air escaping from a tire. Ludwig, who looks like a distinguished gentleman disguised in a stunning German shepherd suit, lies in a patch of sun beneath my skylight and fills the room with manly snores.

And then there's Bea. I found her, a scrawny, frantic beagle, on the road near my house. A later inspection revealed a tattoo in her ear, and I discovered that she had escaped from a medical lab. With her legs flopped out, she sprawls on her back on the oriental rug, makes muffled yips, and pedals her feet. She dreams, I suppose, of chasing rabbits. After the "hunt," she rolls on her side and assumes the shape of a lima bean. The snuffles from the sides of her mouth sound like fingers rubbing a balloon.

These sighs and snores, a gentle background for my work, continue all day. The animals are as much a part of my office as my computer is, but they keep their distance and are busy with their naps. When I write, Bea, Tigger, and Ludwig do not bother me.

That is, they didn't bother me until one hot Indian-summer

day—October 18, 1989. The sultry San Francisco Bay Area weather made me and the animals restless and grouchy. They lay around the room in heaps, then got up, their little nails clicking on the hardwood as they padded to the bathroom and sought the cool relief of a tile floor. Ludwig, panting, shifted repeatedly in his sleeping spot. Bea wanted to be let out, then in, then out again.

After I let her in yet another time and returned to my desk, the house shook violently. The motion knocked me out of my chair and slammed me against a file cabinet. A painting fell off the wall. When a lamp crashed to the floor, I knew I had to run.

We were having an earthquake—not just a few unsettling tremors, but a roller-coaster ride that felt like hanging onto a brontosaurus wrestling with his brother. My animals had apparently sensed this coming. As I dashed to the back door, they skidded across the floor behind me. The ground shuddered and threw us against the walls with a thud. With difficulty, I unlocked the door and pulled it open.

We ran for our lives. Tigger disappeared into the forest. Ludwig, clearly wanting to get as far as possible from our dangerous house, raced to the gate. Bea, who seemed more terrified and confused than any of us, tore halfway up the hill next to the vegetable garden and plastered herself against the fence—perhaps hoping to push her way through it and escape.

My knees knocked together so uncontrollably that I sat on a tree stump to keep from falling. I tried to calm myself as I watched the redwoods sway over my house. I prayed they would not topple onto the roof—and the house would not collapse into a pile of rubble.

In San Francisco, houses *did* collapse. A piece of the Bay Bridge even fell into the water. And calling 911 often brought no help. To make matters even more unbearable, Dan Rather kept tormenting residents by reminding them that the earth-quake was not "The Big One," in spite of being 7.1 on the Richter scale: We had worse in store for us in the days ahead.

Still, at the time I knew none of this. My electricity and tele-phone were out, and I had no way of reaching the outside world. My husband was away on business in southern Califor-nia. I had no close neighbors. In other words, I could have screamed forever, and no one would have heard me. I was liv-ing out my greatest childhood fear: being in a desperate situa-tion, terrified and starkly, irreversibly, alone.

I sat on a tree stump until the brontosaurus seemed to make peace with his brother. Then I gathered my courage, went into the house, and filled the bathtub with water in case aftershocks broke the pipes. With a wrench I tried to turn off the gas but could not tell if I'd succeeded. While I picked up books that had fallen from their shelves, I looked for damage. (Only one new crack had appeared in the mortar between the fireplace bricks.) My knees kept knocking as I went about my tasks, and every few minutes I ran outside just to stand in the open and reassure myself.

By evening the animals came to the patio and ate the din-ners I had set out for them. For myself, I heated tomato soup on the camper stove. Because I felt too afraid to eat or sleep indoors, I placed a rubber mattress and sleeping bag on the patio, well away from any trees and walls that could tumble down. I placed Bea's and Ludwig's pillows close to my bed and climbed, fully clothed, into the unzipped bag—the better to run in an emergency. Tigger perched on the wall bordering the patio. The dogs plumped themselves up on their pillows.

As I closed my eyes, the ground rumbled with aftershocks, but I told myself over and over to count my blessings. The ani-mals and I were safe. The house could have been destroyed, but it was fine. Even so, I continued to tremble so deeply inside that my bone marrow seemed to slosh around in little waves.

My mind filled with images of looters, who were surely roaming the streets that very minute looking for a house in which a woman would be alone, defenseless. They would break down the front door, kill my pets, carry off my grandmother's silver pitcher, and then, dear God, do unspeakable things to me. I would lie helpless on the patio, bleeding profusely from my wounds, while the men escaped in their car. I could never say good-bye to my husband, who would return from his trip to find vultures feasting on my entrails.

To defend myself against my imagination, I opened my eyes and watched the lovely, silver moon. I wrapped my arms around my body for security and told myself I wasn't alone: God was with me. I prayed for calm. Yet I could not be at peace—the terror of the earthquake was still too recent. I couldn't remember ever feeling so alone.

Then Tigger wandered over from her perching spot, butted her chin against my cheek, and settled in the crook behind my knees. Ludwig left his pillow, lay down on the patio, and curled his body protectively around my head. And Bea—who had been so abused that I'd had to teach her what love was—shoved her nose under the cover and rooted into the sleeping bag. She pressed against my chest, rested her head on my neck, and cuddled up. Her gentle, meaty breaths warmed my skin.

I was certain that my pets were worried about me and wanted to help. I knew right down to those waves in my bone marrow that the animals had not come to *get* comfort but to *give* it. They wanted to be sure I was all right.

As we huddled together, I felt safe. The comfort my animals offered seemed different from their normal daily affection. That night their comforting was spiritual, an epiphany for me, one of the a-ha! moments that Fritz Perls described, when people suddenly understand something and are never the same again. I realized that I could give up my childhood fear: As long as I had pets who clearly cared so much about me, no matter what happened, I would never be alone. I might be traumatized, as I had been that day, but if my animals were there, I would have all I needed to get through what was asked of me. The Lord provided—in the form of warm, furry bodies that encased noble spirits. That truth was so simple, yet so profound.

from THE COMPASSION OF ANIMALS

Doing What's Best for SuHana

BONNIE COLEMAN

It was a golden May day when Mom called from an upstairs window: "Bon, look in the pasture. Your baby's here."

I ran to the fence and saw our mare leading her newborn foal, a filly with white stockings and a white blaze down her face. When the young one caught sight of me, she left the mare's side and trotted knock-kneed over to me as though eager to check out a nine-year-old girl. I ran my fingers over the foal's fuzzy dark-copper coat and through her silky mane, laughing and crying at the same time.

"Thank you, Lord. She's just perfect." I named her SuHana.

Leaning my head against her flank, I daydreamed about riding her in parades and shows when she was grown. What a pretty picture we would make! Every day I watched the pony and her mother run around the paddock. Then, a few weeks after her arrival, as my beautiful pony pranced along, she caught her left hind leg on barbed wire fencing. I stared in horror as blood gushed, spattering the dry dust of the corral. Young as I was, I knew what such a deep wound probably meant.

Mom raced to call the vet and I led SuHana into a stall

where she could be treated. Dad told me to wait in the house till the doctor was done.

I paced back and forth in the kitchen along a yellow band of sunlight on the white tile floor. *God, please take care of her,* I prayed. *She's your horse and I want her to have a good life.*

Finally Dad strode into the kitchen. He sighed and crossed over to the sink to wash his hands. "She's hurt bad and most people would have had her put down," he said. "SuHana's going to need a lot of care, Bonnie. I have ranch work to do, so she'll be up to you."

I threw my arms around him. "Thank you, Dad. I'll do everything. Don't worry."

I raced to the barn, my legs flailing like a colt's. In the cool shade, I bent down to look at SuHana's leg. Her wound was stitched and neatly bound. She pressed her head against my chest and softly blinked her eyelashes. It was as if she felt the same relief I did.

Each day for the next few months I unwrapped, washed, medicated, then redressed SuHana's injury. As she grew I adjusted the sling and stanchion my father had rigged to take the weight off her injured leg. Each time I came into the barn she greeted me with her characteristic high- to low-pitched nicker.

The leaves were just starting to change color when Dad came to the barn one evening as I was settling SuHana in for the night. "You've done good, Bonnie. I think SuHana's well enough to turn out to pasture."

The next morning we were both silent as Dad opened the pasture gate and I unclipped the filly's lead. She took a few tentative steps through the gate, then glided away as if on the wind. "Thank you, Lord," I whispered.

Training SuHana was a joy. Her ears perked up at my commands and she seemed to relish the restraint and guidance of the lunge line. After each session she gave me her high-low nicker, a wiggly lip, and gently nudged me back a step. Finally the day came when I rode her for the first time. Her muscles rippled under her sleek coat and she trotted so smoothly it felt as if we were floating. I could hardly wait to ride her in a show.

SuHana's limp slowly disappeared, but not the deep scar from the accident. SuHana refused to let it heal. She bit at it so much we had to call the vet back to bind her leg up again. Still, SuHana seemed unable to leave the wound alone. She kept worrying it, nipping at it and messing it up almost as bad as when she had first hurt herself. After the vet finished binding her leg yet another time, Dad took me aside. "Bonnie," he said, "I'm sorry, but this can't go on. We can't afford a horse that constantly maims itself. We're going to have to find another home for SuHana."

I was devastated, but I knew Dad was right. Few ranchers would have tolerated the expense SuHana had already caused our struggling ranch. When a former 4-H leader of mine agreed to take SuHana, I knew I had to let her go. I took her sweet head in my hands and kissed her forehead. "I'll never forget you, SuHana," I told her. I could barely stand to look as she was led away into a trailer and out of my life.

As the months passed, I heard stories about SuHana: She had become hard to handle; she had had to be sold to another farm; a man who suffered a broken leg working with her had labeled her "a lame outlaw." Every time I heard or thought of her, I prayed, *Please, God, take care of SuHana.*

At dawn one muggy morning shortly after SuHana would have been three, I was jarred awake by a dream. It started out with happy images of my time with SuHana, then darkened with memories of our goodbye, She gave a nicker, but it was filled with fear. *Dear Lord,* I prayed, *I know SuHana's in dan-*

ger. She's your horse. Please protect her and let her purpose be fulfilled.

Shortly afterward Dad gave me a half-Arabian, half-quarter horse to ride in 4-H events, but I could not stop wondering about SuHana. Was she all right? Would I ever see her again?

That summer I entered an out-of-town 4-H show. Following my event, I was carrying a pail of water to my horse when I happened to look toward the riding ring. SuHana! There was my beloved dark-copper filly being guided skillfully through her routine by a girl about my age.

At the end of the event I rushed over to them. I was greeted by SuHana's high-low nicker, as cheerful as ever. I explained to the curious rider—who introduced herself as Lynne—that the horse used to be mine. She hung on my every word, obviously as fond of SuHana as I was. My old filly's coat was gleaming, and Lynne had somehow prevented her from damaging her leg further. When I told Lynne about the dream I had had in June, she looked startled. "That was just around the time Dad and I found her at Red's Sale Yard. The foreman said she was so mean she'd broken a man's leg. But there was something about her I liked and we decided to take a chance on her. If we hadn't bought her she'd have gone off to the dog-food plant that afternoon."

Lynne and I joined the same saddle club and soon became friends. Yet my happiness when Lynne and SuHana won events at riding competitions was always clouded by a nagging sense of envy and unease. Wasn't SuHana *my* horse after all?

The following summer, our saddle club was given a high honor. The members with the three highest ratings—based on performance, appearance and attendance—would get to ride in Portland's annual Rose Festival Parade. For an Oregon ranch girl it was a dream come true. Lynne was chosen as a rider, and

I was named an "alternate princess," which meant I wouldn't get to ride unless someone dropped out. I was glad for Lynne and SuHana, but disappointed for myself.

Then a week after the selections had been made, one of the leaders of our saddle club telephoned me. "Bonnie," she said, "we made a mistake when tallying points for the parade. It turns out Lynne hasn't attended as many events as you have, so you get to ride instead." She waited for my reaction. I guess she expected me to whoop in delight.

But I didn't. In an instant all my mixed feelings of the past year were resolved. All along I had been asking God to take care of SuHana, to help her fulfill her purpose. And he had done that beyond my wildest dreams. Now I had the opportunity to help SuHana step out in her moment of glory.

"Lynne should ride in the parade," I said. "Lynne and SuHana." What a pretty picture they would make!

Finally I understood something I had said before without really comprehending. SuHana was God's horse—and it didn't matter *who* rode her because she was always in his care.

Remembering Rufus

C. W. GUSEWELLE

Twelve autumns we traveled the fields together, and were prodigal with our time. Almost to the last we did not consider endings.

He flew the fences. I clambered ungainly over. He plunged boldly into the thickest, prickliest cover, while I took the easy way around the edges.

"The pup has *style*," a man once said, and I thought I'd won the lottery. He also had much courage, and a ruling passion. If I'd ever gone at writing with a dedication like that, there's no knowing what work I might have done.

"He'll live in his house outside," I told my wife when we brought him home. "He'll be a hunting machine." That lasted until the weather cooled. Then of course he joined us and the old dog and the cats indoors. He slept in a chair or beside the bed. But when we returned from an evening out and he met us at the door with that look of innocence, we knew there'd be a warm place on the covers where he'd trespassed. He could be devious. A sandwich unattended for a moment would vanish in a gulp. His lust for bagels was indecent.

But those were merely vices.

His abiding devotion was to the hunt. He marked the season's turning, and when the alarm sounded in the dark of a

November morning, he always *knew*, and was waiting already beside the downstairs door.

His eyes, gold when he was young, deepened to chestnut brown. A knee failed and had to be repaired. He hunted on it eagerly as ever, not seeming to mind the price of soreness afterward. Then the cataracts began to come, but it was his nose that brought the important messages, and the nose still was keen.

Nearly every man who ever walked behind him spoke of someday wanting a Rufus pup, and several had them or have them now. One of those was Fred Kiewit, who, in the year when we were in Paris saw to it that the autumn was not wasted. Fred is gone, too, now. As is that other fine man, Stuart Mitchelson, for whom Rufus pointed and brought to hand the last bird just at the mellow sundown hour of the last day Mitch and I had together. All of them—those men and Rufus—had full lives, good lives. And good lives never are long enough. But in the end there are some things that medicine cannot fix.

He passed his last night at home, on a pallet in the kitchen, with me beside him. He was tired, and had borne enough, and had been too good a friend to hurt any longer.

In the morning, then, I dressed for the hunt—put on my boots, and folded my canvas coat beside him, with the bird smell still in it. Also his leash. His head came up from the blanket. He'd have stood if he could. All the old excitement was in his eyes.

Dan, who'd cared for him so well from earliest puppy days, made the sad house call. Came to kneel with me beside him. And just as I let Rufus take the quail wing from my hand, released him to wherever it is that old gun dogs and those who've followed them finally go.

With my wife and a daughter I drove to the farm, and on a day of false spring, working together under a warm sun out of season, we buried him, wrapped in the coat, facing a thicket in which he almost always found a covey.

My theology is a bit shaky, and I don't profess to know what, if anything, lies beyond the darkness. But I believe in covering all the possibilities.

So before we walked away, I looked a long minute straight up into the cloudless deeps of that sweet springtime sky and said, in my heart if not actually aloud, *Freddy, Mitch, I'm sending you a pretty good dog. But he isn't* given, *only loaned.*

from THE RUFUS CHRONICLE

"Suzy, Sit!"

PHYLLIS HOBE

When people who don't know me see me walking my dog Suzy, they often go the other way. Suzy is a Rottweiler, weighs more than one hundred pounds and, as a friend put it, "looks very intimidating." Actually, she's a giant puppy with a loving disposition, but not many people want to get close enough to find that out.

Not long after I got Suzy, on our morning walks we began to meet a woman walking her Golden Retriever. We both pulled our dogs in close to our sides, and as they passed each other, the fur on their backs went up. That bothered me because that wasn't like the Suzy I knew. So I decided to take a bit of a risk. The next morning, as my neighbor and her dog approached, I stopped, put Suzy on a "sit" command and asked, "Do you think it might be a good idea for our dogs to get to know each other?"

The woman smiled and said, "I certainly do."

The dogs got along wonderfully, and so did their two owners. Now all four of us look forward to our morning meetings.

Every now and then I come across people who intimidate me because they seem to be more confident and capable than I am, so I make no attempt to know them better. I stick to my own side of the road. But the next time I feel intimidated, I'm going to take a risk. I'm going to say hello and hold out my hand. I might discover someone who's just like me—a person. And instead of making a fool of myself, I might make a friend.

Priorities

TERRI CRISP

$\mathbb{T}$he conditions were ideal for a fire.

The parched hillsides that outline the San Francisco Bay area provided the fuel, and the hot gusts of wind would breathe life into the flames. It was a dangerous combination.

On Sunday, July 7, 1985, an arsonist lit the match—the only missing ingredient—and ignited a disaster.

It started as a small fire in the mountains above Los Gatos. Fire crews responded quickly and predicted an easy containment and no property damage. The fire prompted little concern among the residents of this mountainous community as they went about doing what they normally did on a Sunday afternoon. After all, fires, earthquakes and mudslides were part of the way of life in the mountains, the price one paid for seclusion.

Monday morning, as usual, the mountain dwellers descended from their wooded enclaves for jobs in the valley below as the winds picked up and the temperature climbed into the nineties. By the end of the day, the Lexington Hills fire had been upgraded to a major wildfire.

When the residents of the area tried to return to their homes after work, they were stopped. No one could go back. At the roadblock, there were many emotions—fear, anger, despair and panic. Many people were frantic with worry about their pets.

I was one of the volunteers who made up the animal rescue team in our area. As the rescue team made its way to the front of the crowd at the roadblock, we hoped that the police would let us through. When they finally agreed to let us go into the area to look for pets, we set up a table at the Red Cross shelter and began the process of taking descriptions of pets and addresses.

We worked as late as we could that night and returned at daybreak to continue. It was a large area and the fire was spreading—almost faster than we could move to stay ahead of it. But we just kept going. A grueling ten hours had passed since I'd arrived that Tuesday morning. With a few hours of daylight left, and my van empty of rescued animals, I decided to make one last check at the Red Cross shelter. No one had yet told us that we couldn't go back for more animals.

A woman ran up to my van before I'd even parked. She appeared to be in her mid-thirties, with a smooth, blonde page-boy that framed wide, anxious eyes. I knew she was searching for a pet.

She grasped the bottom of my window frame as I stopped the van and blurted out, "Please, miss, can you help me? I gave my address to one of your colleagues yesterday, but I haven't heard from anyone. It's my kitten. She's only eight weeks old. The poor thing must be so . . . frightened." Her voice broke as she spoke.

"Why don't you give me the information again, and I'll see if I can find your kitten," I told the woman as I pulled a blank piece of paper from my notebook. "Where's your house?"

"Aldercroft Heights. A fireman told me early this morning there were still some houses that hadn't burned."

I could see the hope in her face. But I knew that when the wind changed that afternoon, the fire had headed back in the direction of the Heights—probably to burn what was left.

"My house isn't very big. You could search it in less than five minutes. The kitten likes to lie on the rug in my sewing room, especially when I'm in there working." The recollection brought more tears to the woman's eyes.

Her expression was a mirror image of all of the other displaced people with whom I'd had contact in the past two days. I wanted so much to help them, to ease the anguish and frustration.

"What's the quickest way to your place?" I asked, looking at my map.

The woman used her finger to point out the best route. As she gave me directions, I asked for landmarks. By now a lot of the street signs had melted.

"Okay. I think I have what I need," I said, attaching the paper to my clipboard. "Oh, one last thing. What's your name?"

"April. April Larkin."

I followed April's directions without getting lost. As I got closer to Aldercroft Heights, I could see that the homes I'd passed the day before were now gone. All that remained standing were the chimneys. As I wound up the steep hillside, my gut told me what I'd find. There was no way April's kitten could have survived this inferno.

April had told me her house was exactly one mile up from the horseshoe curve. I watched my odometer. Eight-tenths. Nine-tenths. I was getting close to the devastation. Too close. What I saw made me want to close my eyes. I stopped the van and covered my mouth with my hands.

The house was gone.

I leaned my head back against the car seat and stared at

the ceiling. Tears ran down my cheeks. This was hard . . . really hard. I don't know how long I sat there. But before I left, there was something I knew I had to do. I'd have to look for the kitten. Unfortunately, there wouldn't be a live kitten to place in April's arms. She had told me she'd wait at the Red Cross shelter until I returned. How could I tell her the kitten had died, much less that her whole house was gone?

I knew I didn't want April to see whatever remained of the kitten when she returned. I had to find it and bury it. I got out of the van and forced myself forward.

Through my boots I could feel the heat from the blanket of ash as I wandered through what had once been a home. I used my shovel to poke my way through the rubble. There was so little left, a teacup handle, a twisted metal frame, a chipped ceramic vase—but no kitten. My search seemed futile.

I was on my way back to the van when I heard something. I stopped, but all I recognized was the sound of an approaching helicopter and the persistent wind. After the helicopter passed over, I remained by the van, listening. Hoping. Was it a kitten I'd heard? I suspected not. It had to have been my wish for a miracle that teased my ears.

No! I was wrong. Somewhere nearby there *was* a cat, crying for help.

About then the helicopter was passing overhead on its return trip to scoop more water out of Lexington Reservoir, to douse the southern flank of the fire.

"Get out of here! Move!" I screamed in frustration at the noisy 'copter. "Move!"

It seemed an eternity before it was quiet enough to be able to hear the faint meow again.

"Here, kitty kitty kitty!" I called frantically before the helicopter returned. "Please, where are you?" I moved in no spe-

cific direction, hoping to hear again the meow that would lead
me to the cat.

There it was . . .

The cry for help was coming from the dried-up creek bed
across the road. I dropped my shovel and ran, tripping over
blackened bricks and mutilated pieces of metal. At the charred
edge of the creek I stood still and listened. My heart was beating fast and my hands were shaking.

"Here, kitty kitty kitty!"

"Meooooow."

Across the creek was the wasted remains of an alumi-
num ladder, lying almost submerged in ash. The sound had
come from there. When I reached the ladder, I gasped. There,
huddled next to the first rung, was the tiniest soot-covered kitten I'd ever seen. With the bluest of eyes, it looked up at me
and meowed.

"Oh, you poor thing. Come here." I reached down and
carefully picked up the kitten. Holding it in midair in front of
me, I saw that her whiskers were singed and her paws burnt . . .
but she was alive.

"Is your mom going to be glad to see you," I said, as I cuddled the kitten in my arms. Several times I moved her close
enough to kiss her dirty pink nose. I could feel her fur dry my
tears. The kitten continued to meow, but it was a relieved
meow. She knew she was safe.

When I got into the van, I grabbed an extra bandanna and
poured some water on it. I laid the damp cloth across my lap
and placed the kitten on it. Immediately she started to lick the
bandanna, sucking up some of the moisture. It had been three
days since she'd had anything to drink or eat. I waited to feed
her, not sure how much I should offer her.

As we descended from the Heights, the kitten began to

purr. I stroked her forehead, and tiny blotches of white fur began to appear through the black coating. She had started to groom herself but I tried to discourage her. Ingesting that much soot couldn't be good for her. Within a few minutes, the kitten was asleep.

As I got closer to the Red Cross shelter, I began to practice how I was going to tell April about her house. How do you break that kind of news to someone?

April was waiting, as promised. As she ran to my van, I held the kitten up so she could see it, and for a while I forgot the house in Aldercroft Heights. I just wanted to savor the joy of this reunion.

"Agatha!" she screamed. "Agatha!"

April was hysterical when I handed the kitten to her through my open window. She couldn't talk. Instead she laughed and cried, and held the kitten tightly against her chest. Agatha just purred.

As all this went on, I got out of the van and waited for the inevitable question. When April began to calm down, I decided it was time to tell her.

"I can't tell you how happy I am that I found Agatha," I said, then hesitated. "I just wish there might've been some way I could have saved your home, too."

"It's gone?"

I nodded. "I'm so sorry, April. There's nothing left." I couldn't hold back my tears.

April Larkin freed an arm and pulled me toward her.

"You saved what was important," she whispered. "You saved what was important."

Her words still echo in my heart.

from CHICKEN SOUP FOR THE PET LOVER'S SOUL

A Prayer for Pyg

JOY KELLEY

"Let's go to the quarry," my husband, Randy, suggested one summer evening. "I saw some wild hogs there the other day that I want to show you."

I stifled a sigh. Much as I like animals, I had to admit watching pigs at the quarry for entertainment was hitting rock bottom. It had been a tough year. Randy had lost his job, and I had just started a new career, so I wasn't earning much. We'd learned to entertain ourselves on a shoestring, and most of the time we had fun. But the financial strain would not let up. God didn't seem to be listening to our petitions, and I was beginning to wonder if he cared about us. My prayers had slowed to a trickle.

We drove out to the quarry. Wild hogs are shy, and I figured we'd be lucky to catch a glimpse of one. I was opening my door to get out and explore when a tiny brown-and-black-spotted piglet came rushing out of the underbrush straight at me. He reared up and placed his miniature front hooves on the door frame, squealing excitedly.

Enchanted, I opened a half-empty carton of milk and gave it to him. He slurped it greedily while I scratched behind his ears. Randy practically had to drag me away. All week, I told everyone I knew about my encounter with the adorable piglet.

I worried whether he was okay out in the wild, especially since we hadn't seen any sign of his mother.

Saturday was my forty-second birthday. That evening Randy led me out to the car. There, in the back, was a large box with "Happy Birthday" written all over it. "Randy, you *promised* not to buy me anything!" I protested.

"I didn't," he said with a grin. Suddenly the box began to shake. I ripped open the top. Sitting there looking up at me was one very bewildered piglet. I scooped him up in my arms.

Pygmalion (Pyg for short) and I bonded right away. I think he considered me his mommy. He even "spoke" to me in a different voice than he used with other people. When I went into the house he stood pathetically at the back door with his snout pressed to the screen until I gave in and went out to walk with him around the backyard. For a while Pyg suffered from some species confusion, but eventually he decided he was a dog. He even learned a respectable bark and playfully chased our corgi, Bubba, through the fields. Afterward he would lie at my feet to get his belly rubbed. Even when I was in a funk, worrying about bills or the budget, he could always snap me out of it just by nuzzling my hand.

About four months after we adopted Pyg, Randy and I came across some tasty-looking fruit in the nearby swamp. Although we didn't know what it was, we decided to let Pyg try one since we had heard pigs wouldn't eat anything poisonous. We were terribly wrong—he got sick immediately after eating the fruit, and before long he could only lie beneath the cypress trees, too weak to lift his head. I called the veterinarian and poison control. They said our one hope was to take Pyg to the vet's office and put him on an IV. But, of course, we didn't have the money.

By early evening, Pyg wasn't responding even to the temptation of his favorite chocolate cookies. I knew he was going to die. All I could do was sit with him so he didn't spend his last hours alone. I thought about praying. *If God didn't care enough to help us all these months we've been struggling, what are the chances he'll bother with a little pig?* I asked myself. But I had to try. For Pyg. I laid my hands on my small friend's body and closed my eyes. "Please, Lord, I'm not asking for much. Make him well," I pleaded.

At first he lay there motionless. I kept my eyes closed and my hands on poor Pyg. Then he stirred and stood up. A minute later he sauntered over to his dish. I watched in astonishment. He took a long drink, then began eating hungrily. It wasn't simply a matter of Pyg starting to get better—he was *healed*, completely himself again.

Eventually our financial fortunes turned around as completely as Pyg's health, though not as quickly. But the most dramatic turnaround, I think, was in my attitude. Now I know God always answers our prayers, in his own time, in his own way. Sometimes faith is learning to wait. If I ever need a reminder, I only have to look out into my backyard at the no-longer-so-little spotted pig sleeping peacefully through the heat of the day under the cypress trees.

As Close As My Shadow

GLADYS TABER

I go into this New Year without the companionship of Little Sister, the small black and white cocker. She was never any trouble and she died with as little trouble as possible, her tired heart just beating into silence. She was a funny little person, shy and retiring, unlike the rest of the cockers who are leap-into-lap-at-once people. When strangers came, she retired under the sofa and just poked a small black rubber nose out. If they were very quiet, non-jingling people, she would eventually emerge and casually enter the social group. If they made advances too soon, she got under the radiator and squeezed flat.

She sat under my desk whenever I typed, with her head on one of my feet. Whenever I looked down, one bright dark eye was looking up at me. When I went in the yard, she heeled beside my left foot, steady as my own shadow. She did not bark at the laundry man. She was neat and tidy and drank her water without spilling it all over the floor as some did. She ate as if she were dining out on Spode china. Her son, Tiki, always spreads half of his meal on the floor and skates around in it.

She had little sense of humor, whereas some of the others felt they had a career as comics. She worked soberly at being a

Utility Dog in Obedience but even when she won her loving cup as top dog, she had no feeling of superiority, whereas the Irish is a born trouper. The only time she moved fast was when I started to go away without her. Then no door, no gate shut quickly enough. She was mule-stubborn about ever being away from me, even when I went to the dentist. Many a time I had to lug her small plump form back from the car and plop her in the yard, and no matter how I explained, she looked betrayed. Then she would take up a vigil on the terrace and just look down the road. In her later years, I got so upset over this that I would have some member of the family take her to the back kitchen and offer her a piece of chicken while I stole out the front door. It never worked. She knew.

Perhaps her outstanding quality was the ability to put up with strange dogs coming in, and I felt this was outstanding when she was so dedicated. Once we had a visiting dachshund and Sister was the only one who even tolerated him. Once we had five Irish setters and in the pandemonium, only Sister accepted the deal. She got quietly under the bed and said nothing. She did not even snap when two very large Irish males opened the back kitchen door and came in to suggest they would be pleased to take up part of my bed. She bore with cats. If the Siamese was in a prima-donna mood, Sister would turn her head and stare in the other direction.

She was beautiful only to me, for she was a small old-fashioned cocker, nicely put together but no glamour girl. Visitors who came exclaimed over the rest of the cockers, but only the discerning noticed her peering thoughtfully from under the couch. Non-dog-lovers who came never knew there was a dog in the house, for we simply put the rest in the kennel and let Sister alone. She minded her own business even if broiled chicken was going around. For one thing, she knew I always saved her a really adequate helping of whatever I had. After everyone had gone, however, if I did not set her plate down at once, she nudged me. Her small muzzle would bang against me indicating she had waited long enough.

Possibly I could sum it up by saying Sister was a gentle-woman. But who can ever sum up one small cocker who inhabits one's heart? I can only be grateful that I was privileged to have her for her lifetime, and quite sure she is no farther away than the floor under my desk as I write this.

from STILLMEADOW SAMPLER

Leaving the Fast Lane

LARRY CHAMBERLAIN

$\mathcal{L}$ife in the fast lane held less and less appeal for me by the time I was forty-five, but for some reason I kept it up, day in, day out. Working nights and long hours as a professional chef in Las Vegas led me into an every-evening wildness that would scare even a hardened drinker, which I was. My drinking had become so severe that it finally plunged me into a lonely living terror only a true alcoholic can understand. By the fall of 1991, I had even spent time in a local hospital because of the side-effects from my drinking disease. But I was quickly released, and would soon meet a friend who would change my life completely.

The day my world changed, I was watching the World Series. Drinking helped me to urge on my team. My roommate and his girlfriend came in and told me they had spotted a stray dog at the local convenience store. I'm not quite sure how it happened, but by that evening the dusty-colored, scruffy little dog was fed and resting on the couch in my apartment. He looked like he'd never had a bath or a grooming and I was reluctant even to keep him around. But my roommate piped up, "Can't you just picture him with some eleven-year-old boy, just the two of them knockin' around together?" Somehow, I couldn't get his words out of my head.

A few years before during a physical exam, I had told a doctor about my drinking problem. He told me that I was in the grips of a very serious disease and that there was little he could do to help me. He suggested that I find myself a steady girlfriend and change my lifestyle. If I couldn't find a girlfriend, he told me I should find a dog. "What for?" I asked in surprised ignorance. The doctor said I needed someone or something that needed me.

He must have been right. After "Homer" came into my life, I tried hard to keep up my old habits of drinking and coming home at odd hours, but knowing that Homer was home alone was just too much for me to bear. I started heading home earlier and earlier each night. Homer was so glad to see me! All that affection had an effect on me that was just like magic. Instead of drinking my after-work hours away, Homer and I began wandering through the parks and church parking lots nearby. I made an attempt to find out where Homer came from, but the convenience store owner said that Homer had been abandoned there by transients, so it appeared that the little dog was mine from now on. A visit to the vet and the groomer, plus a new rubber ball, gave Homer a sense of belonging and I took him along with me everywhere. We were seldom apart, and he remains a favorite guest everywhere we go. During a trip to Arizona to visit my daughters, I missed Homer so much that my drinking problem suddenly worsened. At that point, however, I was finally ready for help. My girls called an old friend of mine who introduced me to Alcoholics Anonymous (A.A.), and the program worked wonders for me. But I remain firmly convinced that A.A. was not fully responsible for my recovery. A giant piece of my success had found its way into my heart many months before: my Homer dog. Since Homer and I have become companions I

see a different world than before, a world filled with possibilities, hope, and change. Homer brought something important
to my life. Through my love for him and his unconditional love
for me, change became possible. Maybe Homer brought me
back a piece of the youth I had lost in Southeast Asia or the
trust that I had lost at the end of my marriage. What it comes
down to is that I now have faith in a power greater than myself.

from ANIMALS AS TEACHERS & HEALERS

Loving Jasper

HENRY AND MARY ELLEN KORMAN

Jasper was another lucky "freeway dog." Ken found him when he was about ten months old, dumped on a frontage road. Saving him wasn't easy. "I tried approaching him with cookies and dog food, but every time I got close he snarled at me with a wrecking-yard guard dog kind of look," Ken remembered. He called animal control for help and, when they came, was told the dog was across the border in the next county, out of their jurisdiction. "I had to call the pound in that county and then made three or four trips back and forth trying to get someone to come. Finally I gave up, sat down, and told the dog, 'Bite me!' Instead, he put his head on my lap and rolled over." Ken was sitting on the curb with the dog when the local police arrived. "They told me I had to get out of the road or they would arrest me. I told them I was trying to keep the dog from being run over, which might cause an accident. Then a Burl Ives look-alike who worked for the pound in whose jurisdiction we were sitting showed up. The police said the dog had to go to the pound. 'Burl' said, 'Why don't you just let him take the dog? He's got it under control.' So, I brought him home."

That was just the beginning. He and his wife, Julie Schleisser, had to go to work that night. "I put a leash on him to walk him; he curled up in a ball, peed on himself, and wouldn't move.

I'm thinking 'What will happen to my leather sofa and cash-mere overcoat?' I took all my good clothes, stuck them in the bedroom, closed the door, and said 'Okay, pal, see you later.' I returned to find diarrhea all over the living room and a trip to the Price Club's worth of toilet paper chewed up. I'd brought back a sandwich in a cellophane wrapper, which he grabbed. 'Give me that,' I said, but he growled and ate the sandwich, wrapper and all. I had a monster dog in my house that I thought would kill me in my sleep." The following morning, Ken left the dog at the pound.

However, having been abandoned as a child, Ken could not live with this decision, so after a bad night, he called the next day to ask whether the dog had been claimed. "'No,' they told me. He had gone totally psychotic, snapping at everyone. 'What do you do with a dog like that?' I asked. They told me they keep them for a week and then they kill them. I thought—and I know this isn't the right thing to do—I'd rather leave him in a state park than send him to Auschwitz." Ken went to visit the dog and was told he was vicious. "I leaned against the chain link and he came up to sniff me. I stuck the arm of the sweatshirt that he'd chewed up the first night into the cage. He pulled it in and rolled over, excited and playful. Clearly, he'd once been abused." Ken visited every day until he brought Jasper home again. Five months would pass before Jasper would tolerate other people. "There were times I wanted to kill this dog," Ken said. "But my life changed as I realized what a little love could do for a totally wild crazy creature. He's turned out to be the best dog I've ever had." A little love is exactly what dogs like Jasper haven't had. And by drawing upon a source of love in ourselves, and extending it to them, we may find our own old wounds healed over at last.

from LIVING WITH DOGS

The Dog in the Woods

DIANE WILLS

was brand-new to the real estate business the first time I visited the long-abandoned rural house I was trying to sell for an out-of-state mortgage company. The property was in Brunswick County, N.C., practically in the middle of nowhere. I was putting up a For Sale sign, the hammer echoes blending with the whine of the cicadas, when the feeling struck me: Someone, or something, was watching.

My hammer paused in mid swing. I thought I saw a movement in the scraggly undergrowth behind the house. There it was again. That time I was sure. In the woods was a dog. Even at a distance I could see he was mangy and undernourished. He panted heavily in the thick humidity. Nothing's stickier than a mid August day in coastal Carolina. *I wonder if the house still has running water,* I thought, but one step and the dog melted into the woods without a sound.

While driving back to the office, winding along the dusty country roads, I wondered about the animal. Two weeks before, Hurricane Bertha had walloped Wilmington, tearing a broad swath of devastation. Was that dog a refugee from the nightmare storm? Had he ridden out the gale in those woods?

A few days later I went back to the house to meet with a mowing service to arrange to have the brush cleared and grass cut. Once again I had the eerie sensation of being watched. When I glanced into the woods there he was, in almost the identical spot. I called, "C'mon, boy!" But he vanished at the sound of my voice.

"People shy," the lawn man commented. "You'll never get near him."

I had half a ham sandwich left over from lunch. Pulling it out of my bag I tossed it into the brush, and the dog emerged and pounced on it ravenously. I was able to get a closer look at him. His fur had fallen out in clumps, except for on his head and legs, where it was dull and matted. His back was covered with sores. His eyes shifted furtively. He gobbled my offering, then was gone.

That night at dinner I mentioned him to my husband, John. "It's best you stay away from him," John advised. "Probably wild."

"But he must have belonged to someone once," I protested. I just couldn't understand how anyone could abandon a dog.

"Don't get any ideas," John warned. "We've got a full house." He was referring to our schnauzer, Max, and Minnie, a calico cat. All I could muster in response was a noncommittal sigh.

That week at my Wednesday prayer meeting I hesitated to talk about the dog in the woods. After all, people were concerned with serious life issues—health problems, divorce, finances, job loss. What business did I have asking prayers for an animal? Yet I couldn't get him off my mind. Finally, at the end of the meeting, I said, "I'm sorry if this sounds trivial, but I would like to ask prayers for a stray dog who's living behind a house I'm trying to sell."

To my relief, everyone smiled and nodded. Our minister, Jeff Douglas, rested his hand on my shoulder. "Remember, he's one of God's creatures too," he said.

The dog was put on our regular prayer list. As word got around, he was added to friends' and neighbors' lists as well, and people asked me about him from time to time. A couple of days a week I found an excuse to visit the property, and brought along a bag of kibble and a bowl. I set the food at the edge of the brush and from a distance watched the dog eat. He always seemed tense and hyper-alert, eyeing me warily as he devoured the kibble, backing off if I got close, his fear even more powerful than his hunger. I wished he would trust me not to harm him. Yet I dared not venture too close, afraid of scaring him off . . . maybe for good.

One day John caught me red-handed, loading the trunk of my car with kibble and treats. "Diane . . ." he said sternly. I slammed the lid. "You know we can't take on another pet," he went on. "With my retirement and your just getting started in real estate, we have enough to worry about."

"I know, I just don't want him to starve," I said as I drove off.

The truth was, I didn't know what I wanted. Mainly, I wanted the stray to be all right. I wanted to stop worrying about him. I didn't want him to be so scared of people that no one could help him. I knew we couldn't take in another animal, but I couldn't stand by and do nothing while the poor creature wasted away. *Dear Lord,* I begged, *I feel so bad for that dog. Please help me find a solution.*

Meanwhile, I wasn't having much luck selling the house. At least that allowed me to keep visiting the dog. Weeks passed. I tried to drop by as often as was practicable. Sometimes I saw him and sometimes I didn't. Usually he was skittish and hungry, as if he didn't know how to find food on his own. Then, six weeks after I first spotted the dog in the woods, the National Weather Service issued an alert: A hurricane was bearing down on the North Carolina coast, maybe even bigger than Bertha. *He's all alone out there,* I thought.

We began to prepare for the worst—boarding up windows, stock-piling emergency supplies. One thing I had to do was go around and pull up all my For Sale signs. In gale winds they can become deadly projectiles. As I drove out to Brunswick County, racing ahead of a plum-marbled sky, I was tormented by worry. *He's survived one hurricane. Can he possibly survive another?* How could I convince him to come with me to safety? *Lord, he has to trust me!*

When I got to the house, the rain was coming down in wind-whipped sheets. I didn't see the dog anywhere. After I pulled up the sign I took a bowl of kibble to the edge of the brush. Saying a prayer, I put it on the ground and piled heavy rocks around it. I stood up, the wind buffeting me. One last look.

And there he was, just five feet away, closer than ever before. I stood stock-still even as a clap of thunder crashed overhead. Our eyes met. Then I turned and calmly walked back to my car, opened the trunk, took out a blanket I kept there and spread it out on the backseat. I stole a glance over my shoulder. He was still there. Staring.

I faced the dog. "If you want some help," I said, pointing to the open car door, "please get in."

The trees seemed to bend as one, choreographed by the wind. Then the dog was moving toward me, past me, and nimbly into the backseat.

"Good boy!"

Back home, my husband's resolve broke down as soon as he set eyes on the bedraggled refugee. We put the dog in the bathtub. He was covered with sores and nasty ticks, but he didn't struggle or bite when we washed him, though I knew the soap must have stung something awful. He bore it all stoically. "Good boy," I kept chanting soothingly as I dried him. The storm was poised just off the coast. I took advantage of the respite and rushed the dog over to our vet, Dr. Deborah Wicks.

"Diane," she said, "this dog has the worst case of mange and insect bites I have ever seen. Good thing you got him."

Treatment would be costly, and I doubted John and I could afford it. Right then, I just wanted to get the dog help. "Do what you can," I told the vet as I left. We would decide what the next step was after the hurricane passed. *It's up to you, God . . .*

Rain swept across our driveway as I drove up. John was bringing in camping lanterns and the phone was ringing. I rushed past him to get it.

"Hello?"

It was Dr. Wicks' assistant, Shannon Hewitt. Yes, the dog was doing fine. Shannon was cleaning his sores and giving him a special medicated bath. She thought he was going to pull through okay. "Listen," she said, hesitating. "I don't know if you and Mr. Wills are planning to keep him, but the truth is I've been praying for a dog to come along. Not just any dog, but one who really needs a home and the kind of love my little boy and I could give. This guy here is pretty special. It would be an answer to prayer if I could keep him."

I had to stop myself from crying. Because Shannon worked at the vet's, the cost of treatment would be substantially reduced. John and I could help her out. Together we could swing it.

"What are you going to name him?" I finally composed myself enough to ask.

"After what he's been through, I think I'll call him Gamut."

Gamut made it through Hurricane Fran just fine. Today he has a lustrous coat, as black as coal. He's healthy and he loves people. He couldn't have a better home. When I stop over to visit, he offers me a paw and throws his head back. I know he's grateful because I feel the same way. Grateful for the prayers of neighbors and friends, and for a God who looks after all his creatures.

The Best Part of Our Day

M. J. ARRISON

Frank and I love working in the barn among our goats, and the goats love our company, too. They realize they're in for a day of fun, and they join us, standing right in the way, prancing and bucking, their fur bristling up along their spines. Their playfulness keeps us from getting too serious about this back-breaking job. We allow them to be with us. We talk to them as we go, often giving them one or two gentle bumps as we pass. They are excited. They prance back and forth with us to the big wagon as we dig, and strain, and dump. Their eyes follow every move. Henry rooster clucks his hens over to each new bare spot to check for bugs. They screech and run in chorus, relishing the event. The swallows circle in and out of the barn, flashing blue in the sunlight. "Ke-chee. Ke-chee." We have upset their nesting time. The geese stand at the edge of the activity, necks stretched high, watching. We rake the whole barn floor down to the dirt and sprinkle lime. In one Herculean effort, the work is done in a weekend. We spread the fresh golden straw and stand with our goats to admire our work at the end of the day in the dusty shafts of light.

By the next weekend, after some relatively easy days, we have usually regained our strength enough to empty the litter out of the chicken coop, which is a much easier, but much dustier and less rewarding spring chore.

Later, when I whitewash the walls, all the goats inspect my work. They have to taste-test the mixture which is heavy with lime and cement. At the end of the day you can always tell which goat was the most curious by how much white-wash he's wearing. This year silly black Sable sported a white mustache, a white ear, and splashes of white on his head as testament to how much of a pest he had made of himself throughout the day.

Every May the grass in the lawn grows an inch a minute, and it is almost impossible to keep ahead of it. The vegetable garden is planted, and trees and bushes are transplanted out of our little nursery. Flowers are planted, and then after the deer come, they are re-planted. The pond is treated. The pool is opened. The fences repaired—again. The animal shots are given, the hooves are trimmed, the big wagon mended. Friends come for dinner. Birthdays are celebrated. And we do it all our-selves. We even squeeze in time for a little tennis, and swim-ming, and a bike ride, and usually we have recuperated a bit by the end of June.

On those soft summer evenings in the gathering darkness when Frank and I sat on the porch overlooking the pond, a host of lightning bugs sparkled among the trees. The crickets sawed out their soporific rhythm. The animals grazed in the pasture. We were in heaven.

• • •

THE 11 P.M. PORCH-SIT

A symphony of crickets on a summer's night,
A million fireflies sparkling soundlessly in the trees along
    the streambank,
The moon full, breaking through the clouds,
And a soft breeze about me.

What more peace could God send to me?
How more clearly could He say,
"Rest and calm yourself.
Here is my love for you."

from GETTING MY GOAT

LOVE THAT DOESN'T END

"*I cannot tell my bird to sing
But still I hear her sound.*"

JEFFREY ARMSTRONG

$\mathcal{S}$ometimes we and our best friends have to part. Life may take us in different directions, or we may outlive the animals who mean so much to us. However it happens, losing our best friends is hard to bear. We feel as if a part of ourselves has gone with them.

Yet the love of a best friend never leaves us. Through the blessing of memories, we keep that love alive. As we begin to recall the many beautiful moments of devotion, loyalty, understanding and companionship we shared, our hearts are healed. It's as if God is telling us that best friends will always be together.

Green Eggs and Sam

PENNY PORTER

The egg on our chicken-coop floor was far from ordinary. An ugly mud-green, it looked as if it had been left by some alien creature. Nudging it with my sneaker, I wondered, Where did it come from? Had Mother Nature made a mistake?

"Mama! You found Sam," five-year-old Becky piped up behind me. Holding up her much-read Dr. Seuss book, *Green Eggs and Ham,* she pointed at the scraggly creature on the cover named Sam, then at the egg. "Sam's *in* there," she insisted. "I know he is. It's green."

My husband, Bill, and I and our six children raise cattle and horses on our Arizona ranch. But I'd recently decided I wanted chickens too—and not just everyday Plymouth Rocks, White Leghorns and Rhode Island Reds, which lay white or brown eggs. I wanted Araucanas, the new, amber-gold breed from Chile, which lay rainbow-colored eggs.

I pictured these beautiful eggs hovering in the refrigerator like small, bright balloons, adding magic to our lives. Every day would be Easter.

"Please, honey," I'd said to Bill, "let's order a hundred chicks. I could sell eggs and make a little money."

He looked skeptical but finally relented. I ran for the checkbook before he changed his mind.

Six months later my chicks had grown into fat hens. Brown and white eggs appeared every day. But where were the magical colors? The mud-green egg on the floor wasn't even close to turquoise or sea-foam green, much less yellow or pink.

"Looks like a hand grenade," Bill said as he poked his head into the chicken coop. His words made me feel strangely protective. I cupped the egg in my hand. A curious warmth surged through its smooth, elliptical walls, and it took on magic of its own. What *is* inside? I wondered. There was only one way to find out—wait for it to hatch.

Becky thought "Sam" might be lonesome on his arrival, so we nestled him among three other eggs—two brown, one white—in the incubator in our kitchen. We turned the eggs several times a day, adding teaspoonfuls of water to keep the humidity just right.

On the 21st morning we heard the tapping of tiny beaks against shells. The eggs quivered and rocked. At last the brown and white eggs burst open, releasing three soggy chicks. Becky named them A, B and C. But the green egg stopped moving. "Mama!" Becky cried. "Sam gave up!"

"No, honey. He's just resting."

Tears welled in her eyes. "He can't get out. He's gonna die!"

Pressing the egg to my ear, I could hear mournful cheeps inside. *Was the shell too thick?* I wondered. *Should I help?* Poultry books say "never interfere" because "no hatch" is often nature's way of ridding a species of the weak and the imperfect. But I had a child with dark eyes pleading, "Mama, do something."

Praying I was doing the right thing, I cracked the egg open. A tiny gold beak popped through. Seconds later, Sam rolled out, a scraggly female chick with pure-white eyes embedded like seed pearls in ash-gray down.

"She's blind," Bill said. "You'd better get rid of her now before the other chicks peck her to death!"

I knew Bill was right. Chickens peck at anything in their search for food. Even if Sam survived "peep-hood," a blind chicken could never bluff her way past the knifelike beaks of full-grown hens.

I sensed something special about Sam, however. When she nestled in my hand, she dozed peacefully, enjoying the warmth of my palm like a baby bird beneath its mother's wing.

Since chicks eat and drink at frequent intervals, I decided to find out if Sam could locate food without the noisy cheeping of A, B and C to guide her. When she was four days old, I placed her on the kitchen table about a foot from a soda-bottle cap full of mash. Seconds later, she scuttled toward the mash and pecked up every speck.

Maybe, just maybe, Sam could live a life of her own. And since I was responsible for that life, I had to keep her safe. I put her in a wire cage on the porch.

As time passed, the children took Sam out frequently. They laid her in a doll buggy on her back, claws skyward. Sam remained content while the girls danced around singing. "I am Sam. Sam I am."

One afternoon Becky said, "Sam likes to ride on the swing, Mama." Indeed, wings outstretched, ghost-eyes wild, our Araucana chick clutched the rim of the rubber tire Bill had tied to a tree. "She thinks she's flying," three-year-old Jaymee squealed, giving a too-hard push that tossed poor Sam to the ground. But she was on her feet instantly, flapping her wings and staggering back toward the children's voices.

When the girls tired of the fun, Sam crouched on the porch alone, as though trapped within invisible barriers she dared not go beyond.

Early one April morning, a stray Siamese cat arrived at our kitchen door. His body was so starved it hung over my arm like an empty sock. But what fascinated me was the nonstop purr, even as he slept. The girls named him Ping-Sing, and were delighted to have two pets to play with. Although Sam was safe in her cage, Ping was still a cat that ate birds, and I warned, "Be careful when you take Sam out of her cage. Make sure Ping is outside."

The day came when I overheard Becky say, "Jaymee, maybe Ping and Sam could be friends."

Too late to protest, I peered out on the porch to see Becky shoving two-month-old Sam toward the cat. The Siamese purred like a chain saw, hot glitter blazing in his eyes. The young chicken approached, bewitched by Ping's strange vibration. Nose met beak, and Sam stabbed. Ping recoiled, instantly subdued. By afternoon Ping and Sam were wedged side by side in the doll buggy, enjoying a friendship ride.

To our amazement, Sam began to shadow Ping as radar tracks a distant object. When Ping lay down on the stoop, Sam nestled nearby. When Ping got up to drink water, so did Sam. The two became inseparable, and our blind chicken happily discovered life beyond the cage.

Meanwhile, as my hens continued laying eggs, all the colors I'd dreamed about filled my basket to the brim. I watched for more mud-green eggs, but never found one.

Then January cast a shadow on little Sam's life. Seeing the sign at the end of our road—ARAUCANA EGGS FOR SALE—a passer-by stopped and bought three dozen in assorted colors. He was ready to leave when he glanced at Ping and gasped, "Where'd you find that cat?"

"He found us," I said, "and Sam can't live without him." But Ping was already cradled in the old man's arms. "His name's

Elvis," he said. "Can't stop singin'—in case you didn't notice."

I choked back useless arguments and waved good-bye to Ping.

Now Sam's lonely battle with life began in earnest. Cheeping the loss of her Siamese friend, Sam paced in her cage. She stopped eating. When I saw too many castoff feathers blanketing the cage floor, I worried. I let her out, hoping for a miracle.

At first Sam hunkered down near the porch. One day her curiosity drew her toward the sounds of my free-roaming flock, but angry ducks and stabbing beaks forced her to flee.

Several weeks later, we watched her wait for the hens to go to their nests. Then, squeezing cautiously through the trapdoor into the coop, she found the grain in the feeder.

When night came, however, I still gathered up Sam and put her back in her cage. She'd snuggle with pleasure in my arms. But as the weeks passed, I noticed a resistance each time I carried her off. Then came the unexpected peck on my wrist. Was she telling me to leave her alone?

One summer evening I was later than usual locking the coop for the night. To my surprise, Sam was roosting on the feed trough, sound asleep. She looked so content I left her there. At last, she was one of the flock, ready for life on her own.

By her second September, Sam still hadn't laid an egg. At the same time she became obsessed with a hole between the railroad ties that supported the bucket of Bill's tractor, parked next to the chicken coop. As the days grew cooler, and bobcats, coyotes and raccoons left telltale tracks along Sam's favorite paths, she seemed to find this to be a warm, safe hiding place.

One October night I awoke to screeches of terror from my flock. I grabbed my flashlight and Bill's rifle and dashed outside. In the beam of my light glowed the eyes of a raccoon inside the coop. As the raccoon prepared to rip off my rooster's head, I fired a shot into the air. He fled.

The next morning at breakfast, Becky asked, "Did he get Sam?"

Cold fear gripped me. I didn't know. I'd long ago stopped worrying about leaving Sam with the flock.

We hurried to the barnyard. Near the tractor, golden feathers lay scattered like fallen leaves. "Oh, Mama," Becky said sadly. "Sam's gone."

"Maybe she's underneath," I said to Bill. He climbed up into the cab. Hydraulics whined, and the giant shovel rose from its resting place.

That's when I saw them: four little mud-green eggs, cradled in a straw-banked nest. A farewell gift from Sam? Maybe I should hatch them, I thought. But this was not to be.

Who, after all, could replace her? As she scuttled bravely to the edges of her unseen world, Sam, a mere chicken, had demonstrated how extraordinary life is.

from THE READER'S DIGEST

A Lived-In House

GLADYS TABER

$\mathcal{R}$ecently a friend wrote me asking whether she should buy a cocker. In a way, she would like one, but wouldn't shedding be a problem? And wouldn't it track in dirt?

I was reminded of an aunt of mine who was a dedicated housekeeper. When my cousin and I would get the toys out in the playroom and set up an elaborate village, and fix an imaginary grocery store up with dried beans for money, we never dared go to the kitchen for a glass of milk. If we did, we would come back to find everything put away in the cupboards, and all our work in vain. After a time, my cousin said sadly, "I guess it's no use getting anything out. Let's just sit on the porch."

I also reflected that when my Connie and Jill's daughter and son were small, I often felt tired and frustrated because they cut paper dolls all over the front room sofas, spilled watercolor paint on the good rugs, and strewed toys so quickly that walking across any room was a hazard. But an immaculate house would have been lifeless, and even when I was most discouraged because every crack in the old floorboards was suddenly full of B-B shot, I still felt a house was for living.

The best way to keep a house spotless, of course, would be not to inhabit it at all, but just come in twice a week and clean and then shut it up. I have seen houses that look like that, so guests hardly dare sit down for fear they'll unfluff the sofa pillows. To me, a lived-in house is better. But it is all in what you consider important.

As I went back to my friend's letter, I thought about life with dogs. Well, Holly filches a milk carton from the trash can and tears it up in the keeping room. Jonquil pads in from a mole hunt and leaves fresh dirt on the clean floor as she wags with pride. Especially Me brings in a crop of stick-tights and Linda always manages a few briars. And Tiki can't help it if he waded in a puddle in that low spot in the yard.

For us, the love and companionship of the cockers and Irish compensate fully for any minor discomforts in house-keeping. But as far as my friend was concerned, I advised against a dog. Everyone has to set up his own standard of values, and live by them. And what is important to one person may not matter at all to another. We ourselves found that a frisky crowd of cockers and Irish kept the house from being too silent and too solemn when the children went away to school. We couldn't be melancholy when two dogs tried to get in the television set to see where Lassie was!

Among the many gifts our dogs have given us, I might rate laughter as one of the best. They just naturally do funny things, from jumping in the air after wasps or grasshoppers to tunnel-ing under the border after moles. The cockers never realize when they are funny, but the Irish has a gleam in her dark eyes as she knocks out a screen and leaps in. Didn't think I could do it, eh? she says.

If she decides she is tired of regular dog meals, she sits by her pan and barks until we rush out, then she moves majesti-cally to the refrigerator and points. There's something better in there, she indicates. She gets it.

The dogs make cooking more fun. I love to cook, but I am

not a lonesome-minded woman. I like to do a cheese soufflé with four helpers who snap extra bits of cheese and wag wild tails when I beat up extra eggs. Cutting up chicken or turkey leftovers is a very social occasion at Stillmeadow. I am not alone. Who could feel neglected with at least six companions bouncing about?

They also help when I am typing. They hop up and look, they lean against me, they comment. They bring toys to lure me away to happier pursuits. And the Irish often manages to re-arrange all my manuscripts when I go out for a drink of water!

from STILLMEADOW SAMPLER

Till We Meet Again

CLEVELAND AMORY

I remember well—as I'm sure anyone who has ever been owned by a cat always does—the first time I knew Polar Bear was seriously ill. I remember it well—as I'm sure you remember when you knew your cat was seriously ill. It is like being stabbed.

I also remember the first time I recognized that it was something far worse than either arthritis or the mere inevitable gradual encroachment of old age. I was playing chess with Ed Kunz—a Swiss gentleman and close friend of mine who lives in the same apartment building. Polar Bear was, as usual, lying asleep beside me on my chair, and I was leaning over to pat him from time to time.

But chess is a very absorbing game, and one time, when I had not looked at him for some moments and reached out to pat him, I suddenly realized he was not there. At almost the same moment—or at least so it seemed to me—he hit the floor. Or, rather, what he really did was to flop to the floor. It was a sad and awful sight. Worst of all, as I picked him up, he looked at me as if to apologize.

Animals battle whatever infirmity or wound or disability they have with such bravery and lack of complaining that it must actually be seen to be believed. I would see that quality in

Polar Bear many times that terrible spring, and I shall never forget it. Every now and then, I would hear one of his small *AEIOU's*—the sound with which I had grown so lovingly familiar—and the only difference I could notice now was that it was a little eerily cut short, until it sounded almost like a plain *ow*. It was not, of course, but that is what it sounded like.

Anyone who has ever been in a position similar to mine and who has seen his or her animal carry on a difficult fight can only love and respect that animal more, particularly when you realize that it takes a very special kind of courage. It takes a courage that is very different from human courage but is, if anything, more worthy of admiration, because human courage comes at least armed with some knowledge, whereas animal courage often comes with no knowledge at all—not even, in the case of disease, knowledge of what it is they fight.

In any case, after that awful flop to the floor, I knew it was high time, and probably past high time, for me to take Polar Bear to the vet.

Polar Bear was, as are almost all cats, extremely wary of a vet office and regarded it at best as somewhere between a Lebanon and an Iraq. Although his vet, Dr. Fred Tierney, could not have been more gentle or considerate, I could tell from his first examination of Polar Bear that he was concerned. When he was finished, I knew from the look in his eye that the news was not good. And it certainly was not. What Polar Bear had was that dreaded age-old disease that eventually afflicts so many animals; uremic poisoning, or kidney failure.

I cannot even now bring myself to go over the day-after-day, week-after-week, step-by-steps Dr. Tierney tested and tried: the treatments that sometimes seemed to make Polar Bear suddenly better and then—equally suddenly, it seemed—failed as well as those that seemed, at first, and oh so slowly, to help a little and then, just as slowly, seemed to fail. Finally, there came the day when Dr. Tierney said quietly, "I am beginning to wonder whether we're doing the little fellow much of a favor."

I did not answer, but I knew the answer.

If there was one thing about which I was determined, it was that Polar Bear should not suffer pain. I hate to see any animal in pain, but for the cat who had probably done as much as any single cat who ever lived for the cause of cats in general and the adoption of strays in particular—and had done it not only in this country but also in nineteen other countries where the books about him were published—for that cat to suffer pain was simply, to me, unconscionable.

The next morning, I sent for Polar Bear's close friends to say good-bye to him—among them every single one of the staff and volunteers from the Fund for Animals office. Each one of them held him in his or her lap and hugged him.

Vets are not always keen on having the owners hold their animal or even be in the same room when their animal is being put down. The reason is that most vets have had experiences with it that do not make it practicable—experiences ranging from hysterics to last-minute changes of mind.

In my case, I was pleased that Dr. Tierney never even mentioned this. He knew, without my saying it, not only that I wanted to be in the room with Polar Bear but also that I wanted to be holding him.

The first injection was an anesthetic, but then before the final one, the sodium pentobarbital, something happened that I shall never forget. Polar Bear was lying on a metal-topped table, and I was holding his head with both my hands. Marian, my longtime assistant, had her hands on him too, but just before the final injection—with what must have been for him, considering his condition, incredible effort—he pushed in a kind of swimming movement on the metal directly toward me. I knew he was trying to get to me, and although Dr. Tierney was already administering the fatal shot, I bent my face down to meet that last valiant effort of his, and with both my hands hugged him as hard as I could.

In what seemed just a few seconds, it was all over. Dr. Tierney did a last check. "He's gone," he said, still quietly. Only then did I release my hugging hold, but as I say, I still remember that last effort of his, and I shall remember it always.

Actually, leaving the room, I was good at first. When I got to the outer office, however, I saw Dorsey Smith—a dear friend of mine and Polar Bear's too—who was holding her own cat in her hands.

"Is it Polar Bear?" she asked me. I nodded. But when she also asked, "Is he all right?" I could not even shake my head. Instead I did something so un-Bostonian and so un-me— something I could not help, not even just in front of Dorsey but with all those other patients there, too. I burst into tears. It was embarrassing, and I was ashamed; but the worst part was that for the first time in my life that I can remember, I could not stop crying.

I have always believed that the best place to bury your animals is in your heart. But at the same time, since so many people knew Polar Bear and wanted to know where he would be buried, I finally gave in. I chose as his final resting place the Fund for Animals' Black Beauty Ranch in Murchison, Texas, which over the years has become home to thousands of abused or abandoned animals.

To Chris Byrne, the able manager of the ranch, as well as to his extraordinary wife, Mary, fell the job of finding the right place, the right headstone, the right plaque. They did it wonderfully well. The plaque is not only a lovely one but also is at the very center of life at the ranch and is in the shade of three trees—a place that Polar Bear loved.

To me fell the job of writing the inscription for the plaque. I did it as follows:

Beneath This Stone
Lie the Mortal Remains of
The Cat Who Came for Christmas
Beloved Polar Bear
1977-1992
Till We Meet Again

What I wrote on Polar Bear's monument I do believe— that we will meet again. And if I do not always believe it, I always try to believe it, because I also believe that if you try hard enough to believe something, you will in time believe it. And one thing I know is that, when Polar Bear and I do meet again, the first thing I will say to him is that he is the best cat ever. And another thing I know is that, wherever we are, he will be the best cat there too.

from THE BEST CAT EVER

The Dog
Who Found Me

JEFFREY MOUSSAIEFF MASSON

When I was living in Poona, near Bombay, in 1968, I adopted a small stray dog who lived with me in a house in Koregaon Park, some five miles from the university where I was writing my Ph.D. thesis. I never took the dog with me to the university. As I prepared to leave India, it was necessary to find the dog a new home, and I was able to set him up with friends who lived some twenty miles away along the bus route that led to the University of Poona. A few days after they took the dog, I was working with my pundit (a learned man schooled in the traditional way) in his office at the university, very early in the morning, when we heard a knock on the door. We were surprised that anybody would be calling so early. When I opened the door, who should be there but my loyal little friend. My pundit was appalled (dogs are considered very unclean to an orthodox Brahmin), but when he heard the story of how this dog had been given away and had now found me, he created a Sanskrit verse on the spot, the gist of which was that I was bound by karmic ties to this little fellow and must never abandon him again.

How did my dog find me? I asked people at the university and was told that somebody had seen him board a bus that went by the road in front of Poona University. But how had he managed to get off at the right stop? This still puzzles me.

from DOGS NEVER LIE ABOUT LOVE

Ginny's First Cat

PHILIP GONZALEZ AND LEONORE FLEISCHER

---

*G*inny and I often used to go back to see her former friends at the animal shelter. Because I was so happy with her, I felt grateful to the shelter. It even occurred to me that I'd ripped them off; I'd given them only ten bucks, and they had given me in exchange a creature who was all affection, who was a good friend and great company. Ginny was the bargain of the century. In my opinion I still owed the shelter. I owed them big.

So I would buy all kinds of cat and dog snacks and take Ginny back there for a visit, and we'd give her old pals in the cages a little treat. Ginny and Kenny were always happy to see each other, and my little dog would make the rounds of the cages, saying hello to old fellow shelter-tenants who were still waiting for homes—her own puppy had been adopted soon after Ginny found her own home—and making the acquaintance of the new arrivals. . . .

It was spring, and spring is kitten season. There must have been forty or fifty cute little kittens waiting for adoption at the shelter. The cages were filled with kittens—mewing, playing, batting at each other's ears, rolling over one another, climbing up the bars of the cage, snoozing—all of them adorable, all of them waiting for good homes.

Ginny ran eagerly from cat cage to cat cage until she saw a very pretty kitten, snow-white with big blue eyes, about ten weeks old. The kitten was a real knockout; she looked like something you'd see on a Valentine card, fluffy and very cuddly. It was obvious that from the minute she laid eyes on the kitten, this was the one Ginny wanted. She began to whimper and actually tried to climb into the cage. I opened the cage door, took the kitten out, and handed her to Ginny. Right away, she began to clean and groom it, exactly like a mother cat. She licked it vigorously, she even nibbled its fur gently with her teeth, the same way a mother cat does. The kitten loved it and showed her approval by purring loudly.

I adopted the white kitten for Ginny and named her Madame. Two days after I took her home, I realized that something was wrong with the kitten. She was affectionate and responsive when she was looking straight at me, but when her eyes were closed, or her back was toward me, she paid no attention to me or my voice. When I spoke her name, her ears didn't even twitch. Most important, when I opened a can of cat food in the kitchen, or rattled her food dish, she didn't come running, even though the electric can opener is the best cat caller ever invented. I had my suspicions, so I walked up behind her and clapped my hands, loud.

Madame didn't cock her ears or turn her head toward the sound. She didn't even flinch; she was stone deaf! I found out later that there is a gene for deafness in white cats with blue eyes, which is why you often see a pure white cat with one blue eye and one yellow or green eye. This is nature's way of protecting the animal against deafness. Usually, deafness will surface in male cats, but in the case of Madame it was a female who was born deaf. . . .

From all the kittens available in our local animal shelter,

Ginny had selected a handicapped cat to save and cherish. I had no way of knowing it back then, but a lifetime pattern was already being set.

I enjoyed watching Ginny as she raised Madame from a kitten. She behaved exactly like a mother cat; she gave up sleeping on my bed and slept instead curled around the kitten, who nestled against her belly, purring loudly, her little paws making bread in the air. I gave them a cardboard box with an old sweater of mine spread out on the bottom to make the box warm and snug, and the two of them used it for a bed. Several times a day, Ginny would groom tiny Madame with her tongue and with the gentle tips of her teeth, and she always watched over the cat when she ate. She never let that kitten out of her sight.

I could swear that Ginny understood that Madame was deaf. She would never approach the kitten from the rear, but always circled around to the front where the kitten could see her. She never barked at her, either; it was as though she knew that Madame couldn't hear her barking.

But the funniest thing was the way Ginny moved Madame around. At first, when the kitten was really small, Ginny would carry her from place to place in her mouth, exactly as a mother cat would. She held Madame gently in her teeth by the loose fur on the back of her neck, and the kitten would dangle, paws in the air, her eyes squeezed tightly shut and her little tail curled up on her belly. She seemed to enjoy being carried, because you could hear her purring in the next room.

But in a couple of months, Madame had grown too big and too heavy for Ginny to carry around, so Ginny took to pushing the kitten across the floor with her nose, exactly like the puck in a game of shuffleboard. Anywhere Ginny wanted Madame to go, she pushed her. The kitten would close her eyes and allow herself to be pushed, as though she thought it was all a game. Ginny kept this up until Madame was full-grown. It was a truly comical sight to see a little white cat gliding across the floor at the end of a dog's nose.

By the time she was three months old, Madame had learned to compensate for her deafness. Nature is wonderful, and nature provided that little white cat with special senses. Her eyesight is spectacular, even for a cat, and she possesses a sense of smell so highly developed that I swear she can smell the cat food right through the can. . . .

In time, Madame learned to "hear" with her body. Although she could never distinguish voices, she could tell if somebody was walking toward her because of the vibrations in the floor. And, perhaps because she lives in a world of profound silence, she is a peaceful and nonaggressive cat, sweet-natured, affectionate, but not exactly of a calm disposition. When she was a young cat, she was a holy terror. Not to people, but to my furniture and possessions.

Madame would swing through the air like Tarzan, leaping from curtain to curtain, tearing them with her claws. She was death to china, lamps, even the poor old VCR, which she landed on from a height of eight feet in the air and knocked down off its table. And she loved to disappear; it was her favorite game. One of her best tricks was to poke a small hole in the cambric underlining of my sofa, enlarge the hole with her paw until it was big enough for her to climb into, and there she would hide, hanging inside the sofa bottom, up off the floor, unseen, as though she were swinging in her own private hammock.

Another time when she was still a kitten, Madame vanished off the face of the earth for more than two hours. I looked high and low for her, with no success. And she couldn't hear me calling, not that hearing would have made any difference. When a cat wants to hide out, it can make itself selectively deaf, even if it wasn't born deaf.

I was at my wits' end. I couldn't remember whether I'd had the front door of my apartment open for a few minutes. If Madame had wandered out, she'd be at a terrible disadvantage. A deaf cat has no business being out on the street; it has no natural defenses against hundreds of possible dangers, like speeding cars or dogs that are not in its line of vision. Automobiles are statistically the nation's biggest killer of cats.

Ginny trotted in from the bedroom, where she had been napping.

"Ginny, go find Madame," I said, not knowing whether or not it would work. But Ginny understands everything; she went straight to the lamp table next to the sofa. There was a lamp on it that Madame had knocked over once and broken a hole in, but because I couldn't afford a new lamp I'd put the shade back on it and turned the hole away toward the wall.

Ginny went up to the lamp and put her paw on it, tapping it twice. At once, little Madame came out of the hole. She had curled up inside the hole, under the lampshade, because the lamp was lit and she enjoyed the heat it generated. The vibrations from Ginny's tapping paw woke her up and brought her out.

Madame and Ginny still have a special relationship; Ginny will defend Madame if any of the other cats try to pick on her, and Madame will still cuddle up against Ginny from time to time, as if asking to be groomed. Ginny, of course, is always happy to oblige, and nibbles and licks Madame's fur.

from THE DOG WHO RESCUES CATS

Rocky

TERRI L. COLLINS

I've put off writing this because I know I will cry as I put the memories on paper. Do you ever stop missing the Greatest American Dog in the World?

My older brother gave Rocky to me in 1979 when I was nineteen years old. An unwanted mutt, the dog was on his way to the pound and only six weeks old. He probably could have had a successful career as a celebrity impersonator, because he looked a lot like Benji; however, he was too busy taking care of me to let such mundane pursuits as stardom interfere.

I'll never forget that very first night when he lay in a box by my bed and cried, missing his littermates. I picked him up and cuddled him next to my heart, where he would sleep for the next fifteen years. We soon became inseparable. I found out at Rocky's initial checkup that he had been born with a congenital heart defect that the veterinarian predicted would get worse as Rocky grew. The prognosis was not good, and we left with a two-year life expectancy looming in front of us.

For some reason, I didn't worry about it. I knew that if I loved him enough, he would live forever; and I was almost right. To the amazement of everyone (except Rocky and me, who never had a doubt), his condition remained the same. It never got better, but it never got worse.

Over the years and all the changes of life, Rocky and I were a team. If I cried, he would bring me his toys and kiss me so much that I eventually had no choice but to start laughing and kissing him back. He saw me through a divorce (the result of a "we were way too young to be married" mistake), and through a failed engagement when I was actually stood up on my wedding day! I would have wallpapered my room with "The more I know men the more I love my dog" bumper stickers had I not met the wonderful man with whom I just celebrated ten near-perfect years of marriage, Shawn.

From the beginning of our courtship in 1985, I made it very clear that Rocky and I were a package deal. Shawn never resented Rocky or his place in my life and he became a great daddy. After our marriage in 1986, Rocky kept his rightful place at night, next to my heart, and between Shawn and me!

In 1986, our family grew when we adopted a stray cat, Cilla. In 1987, we added another stray, Tigger; and in 1989, we adopted Christopher from the animal shelter because he had giant ears and looked like a bat instead of a cat and because it was his last day to be rescued. Rocky adapted well to the new additions, even protecting tiny Christopher from the other cats by walking over him everywhere he went!

In 1993, Rocky was fourteen years old, and Shawn and I were excited to be buying a brand-new home. It was gorgeous; and our down payment was waiting patiently in the bank for close of escrow, when Rocky had heart failure. I rushed him to the vet, who immediately placed him on IVs and put a tube down his throat. She told me that with the right medications and time in the hospital for observation, he could pull through. It was very risky and very expensive, and due to his age, the logical step would be to put him down. I knew that because of the house we were broke. I also knew that Rocky had never given up on me, and I could not give up on him. I called Shawn, and the Greatest Dog in the World proved to me I had the greatest husband in the world.

"Tell the vet to do whatever has to be done to save him. Money is no object," Shawn said. And he continued, "If we have to use our whole house payment we will. We just won't get the house."

I visited Rocky every day in the hospital, and he pulled through. We were still able to get the house, and we settled in.

Rocky was beginning to slow down. He developed cataracts, but could still see well enough to growl from my lap when one of the cats jumped up next to us. He couldn't jump up on the bed anymore, so every night Shawn or I would lift him up so he could take his place between us. He couldn't control his bladder through the night very well, so our new white carpet in the master bath was initiated with yellow, decorative spots. It was okay. How can you value carpet over your best friend?

The Lord blessed us, so I no longer needed to work; and I was with Rocky constantly. When I suffered a miscarriage, he pulled me through. In September 1994, Rocky was fifteen, and a lump on his chest was diagnosed as lymphatic cancer. When the vet said, "Two weeks at most," I remember my knees buckling, and Rocky straining to get out of the vet's arms so he could get to me. Even at his worst hour, he thought only about me. We decided to take him home. He was still eating well and did not appear to have any pain.

From that day on, I never left my house. I realize how crazy this was to most people, but Rocky had never let me go through anything alone, and I would not allow him to be alone when he needed me. If I had to shop or do errands, I waited until my husband got home so he could be with Rocky. I took

Rocky over to see my mom and dad, as he had always loved them so much. It was a special time. Two weeks turned into two months, and we got Rocky his first-ever dog Halloween costume so he could run to the door and greet the kids. When Thanksgiving rolled around, Rocky was still sitting up and begging for scraps he was not supposed to have. By December, I began to leave the house for short little trips to the store, and every time I got ready to leave, I would hold Rocky and tell him over and over again, "Wait for Mommy. Don't go anywhere until Mommy gets home." I repeated this mantra for over five minutes; and although I knew Rocky understood, my human friends would roll their eyes and question my sanity.

I began to pray that Rocky would make it through Christmas; and as the season rolled around, I put his stocking up and took him to the pet store to get his picture taken with Santa. Shawn and I always celebrate on Christmas Eve; so Christmas Eve night Rocky ate his present of prime rib, and we opened his presents for him. The night was perfect, and we had all celebrated one more Christmas together.

Shawn and I always make the hour drive to my parents' for Christmas, and usually Rocky went, but with all the nieces and nephews, we thought it would be too much for him; so I gave him the lecture on waiting for me, as always, and we left.

We were gone longer than planned, the longest I had left Rocky since September. As soon as the garage door began to rise, I began to worry. Usually, Rocky came through the doggie door in the laundry room when he heard the garage and got in the car so he could "ride in" with us. He did not come out, and I ran into the house. I looked at Rocky and he walked up to me, wagging his tail. He put his feet on my leg to be picked up, and I lifted him, looked into his eyes, and told Shawn, "It's time." We sat on the floor, and I held him in my arms, against my heart, as I first had done over fifteen years earlier, trying to comfort him now as I had then.

I started talking to him. I told him how much I loved him and that if his job as a dog was to be loyal and loving and look after me, then he had done the very best job any dog could do. His breathing became shallow, but he kept looking in my eyes; and I realized that, as always, he was worried about me. I choked back the tears and put on a happy voice. I told him, "Rocky, you go ahead and go. Mommy will be okay. When you close your eyes, you'll be able to run fast again and see everything. We'll still be together. We will always be together. Go ahead and go. I'll be okay." He closed his eyes and died in my arms on Christmas night 1994.

The weeks that followed were the worst of my life. All of a sudden, for the first time in fifteen and a quarter years, I was alone. The cats were confused; and Christopher, now five, kept looking for Rocky and crying. Very few people understand the grief involved in losing what to them was "just" a dog but what to you was a *dog,* God's greatest creation and your child; your playmate; your therapist; and above and beyond all else, your very best friend. Rocky enabled me to love everyone and everything around me a little more because of the depth of his love for me, and I know that I could never repay him for all he brought to my life. People always told me Rocky was lucky, but they were wrong. I was the lucky one. I guess in a way I was right fifteen years ago when I thought Rocky would live forever if I just loved him enough. He may no longer be lying next to my heart every night, but he's in my heart night and day, and he will live there forever.

• • •

POSTSCRIPT: *As I write this, Austin Collins is lying on my lap asleep. Shawn and I adopted him from the animal shelter two years ago when he was three years old. He is a purebred apricot poodle (about ten pounds), and his tag said he was given away because "there was no time to house-train him." In three years? He learned in a week and never makes a mistake. (I told him even if he does, we value life and love over carpet in this house, so don't worry.) Austin is here to stay for as long as God chooses to bless us with him. He is very clingy! He never leaves your lap if you are sitting; and if you are standing, he wants to be held. . . . I guess I'd be clingy too if I thought I had a home for three years and ended up looking through bars waiting for my companions to return. Christopher and Austin chase each other all over the house; and after Austin was here two weeks, Tigger finally came out from under the bed! And yes, he sleeps between us. I had not planned to get another dog, but the house didn't feel like a home. At first I felt guilty loving Austin, but I know I wouldn't be capable of loving Austin so much if Rocky hadn't shown me how. I know my story is long, but love is hard to condense.*

from OUR BEST FRIENDS

To Eloise With Love

GARY RICHMOND

Have you ever wondered if animals have the capacity for love? I have been asked dozens of times, and to me the answer is a resounding yes! It's all too evident. Some people, though, are skeptical and want some kind of proof. So without shame I offer it to you. . . .

I saw this love all the time when I worked at the zoo; but it was never more apparent than when Eloise, a three-year-old orangutan, came for a month's stay at the health center.

Eloise had an undiagnosed rash over most of her body. She was as miserable as any patient I have ever seen, animal or human. Her illness turned out to be a type of herpes that would be with her from time to time for the rest of her life. She itched more than anyone can imagine. Of course, scratching just caused more itching. She cried as she scratched and some-times threw herself against the side of her cage and rubbed her body against it, hoping that her itching would stop.

The veterinarians used drugs to alleviate her itching, but almost everything they gave her seemed useless. Only sleep-inducing drugs brought any relief to Eloise. Unfortunately, they couldn't just keep sedating her; that only created a new set of problems.

Eloise needed comfort, but because the herpes virus was

very communicable, we were not able to offer much aid. Some of the staff would put on rubber gloves and simply sit and hold her hand, or they would reach into her cage and rub her back and arms with benadryl or cortisone cream. She would look at us with very loving eyes that pled for more help than we were able to give. There was, however, one remedy that helped more than anything: Eloise had to have her security blanket. She was lost without it. Actually, it was only a bath towel. Fortunately it was a white bath towel, and Eloise could not distinguish one from another, so we could use several different towels daily (for sanitary purposes).

When Eloise was suffering most, she would wrap the towel tightly around her and try to sleep. When she woke up, she would drape it over her head. She looked like a nun (an ugly one, no doubt). There were times when she sucked on a corner of the towel, and when she wasn't doing anything special with it, she just held it next to her body. She was never out of contact with her towel. Even during our daily exchanges she would not let go of one towel until she had a firm grasp on another.

Eloise used towels as a substitute person, just as Linus does in the wonderful comic strip "Peanuts." In the wild, Eloise would rarely have been out of contact from her mother, but in captivity she was raised as a human baby. She was picked up and put down several times a day, and that treatment had taken its toll. She needed her security towel as much as Linus needed his blanket. To say she was attached to her towel would be an understatement. She fell apart if she couldn't have it. This kind of behavior is an example of a love or liking of the subanimal, and it demonstrates that animals can attribute value to an inanimate object.

I am happy to say that the day came when Eloise's virus

abated and she was able to return to her own cage in the collection where she could play with and touch other members of her own species. The day also came when Eloise no longer reached for a towel-companion. She found that she had animal-friends to take its place.

from IT'S A JUNGLE OUT THERE

Cat With No Name

BERT CLOMPUS

The cat showed up a few days after my bookkeeper, Norman, told me he was quitting. Scrawny as a frayed piece of rope and gray as a foggy morning, she sat high atop a bale of hay in my barn, mewing and complaining. That reminded me of how Norman had reacted when I tried handing him a key to my hardware store so he could open up in the morning. "I'm quitting, Bert. I can't handle that responsibility right now," he complained. I looked at my employee's pallid face and frowned. He disappointed me and I told him so. But I excused him from opening up the store and let him get back to his bookkeeping.

I wish I could have ignored Norman's refusal the way I ignored the gray cat. I busied myself filling three bowls for the cats I already had—Faith, Hope and Sheldon. When I was finished, the gray cat jumped to the floor, boldly pushed Sheldon aside and began eating his food. Sheldon, who was twice her size, looked up at me and protested. "Hey," I told him. "I can't fight your battles."

The gray intruder quickly finished Sheldon's food and shouldered Faith aside to get at hers. "I bet I know where *you* come from," I accused. "You come from that cat-infested old barn down the road."

I didn't need another cat. So after she was finally satisfied, I opened the barn door and shouted, "Shoo!" But the gray cat ignored me and nonchalantly climbed back on the bale of hay. That irritated me almost as much as Norman's refusal to take the key.

The next morning the gray cat was still there, staring down at me and informing me how hungry she was. "That's tough," I snapped. I filled my cats' dishes, put them outside the barn, and left. Later, I saw she was outside, pushing my cats aside and attacking their food. And one by one my cats walked away, totally disgusted with her, as I was with Norman.

When the pushy feline finished eating, she tried making friends with my cats. She began rubbing against them, but they either walked away or batted her with their paws. I didn't blame them. Then I—and my 67-year-old temper—picked up a stone and hurled it at her. The cat scooted around the side of the barn.

Immediately I became guilt-ridden and hoped God was busy looking somewhere else. I also hoped it was the last I had seen of the little pest. But the object of my short-lived wrath cautiously peeked at me from the corner of the barn. "Okay, have it your way," I muttered. It was the same thing I had muttered to Norman.

The following morning the gray cat was first to greet me and begin her incessant chatter as she followed me into the barn. There she watched me fill the bowls. There were four now, and she hungrily tore into them. When Faith, Hope and Sheldon finally arrived I had to put more food in the dishes. "Keep this up and you'll eat me out of house and home!" I complained to the gray cat, who contentedly licked her paws. It reminded me of the way Norman had contentedly returned to his quiet world of bookkeeping for me.

However, I soon began looking forward to the gray cat's early-morning greetings down by the hydrant outside the barn. And one morning, while I was retrieving the empty bowls, she quickly rubbed the back of my hand with her cheek and dashed away. It happened faster than the beat of a butterfly wing. A few days later she allowed me to pet her and, finally, hold her. She weighed next to nothing. That cat and Norman were really two of a kind. "Dear Lord," I prayed, "help me put some meat on this poor thing."

Faith, Hope and Sheldon continued to snub the gray cat, which made me more sympathetic toward her. I decided to have my vet check her out. I also intended to have her spayed. The vet told me to put her in a carrier the night before her operation.

When that night arrived, I tried putting her into the carrier, but she seemed to have grown another four legs. It was like fighting a furry octopus. She also began mewing pitifully, as though knowing what lay ahead for her. Her cries broke my heart and made me relax my grip. She got free and disappeared into the night. "Good!" I shouted after her. "I'll never see you again, and things will get back to normal around here!"

The following morning, much to my relief, she was waiting at the hydrant. I bent down to pet her, but she would have none of it. She ate with one eye on her food and one eye on me. And for good reason too—the next time I would show no mercy, and off to the vet she would go.

But my plans for the gray cat evaporated like rain on a hot sidewalk. She was finally putting on weight, but it was all in her belly. After a few days, it became obvious she was pregnant, and I knew then why she had pushed her way into my life. I only wished I knew why gentle Norman had failed me.

"Boy, you sure know how to complicate things around

here," I complained to the gray cat. I was certain this would be the last straw for Faith, Hope and Sheldon, and they would pack up and leave. Nevertheless, I tried building up the pregnant cat for her coming ordeal by feeding her as much as she could consume.

The day finally came when the gray cat gave birth to three kittens in one of the stalls. Two were alive. One was gray and striped like a tiger. The other was carbon-black from the tip of its nose to the tip of its tail.

The kittens remained in the stall for a few more days and then disappeared. I looked everywhere for them, but couldn't find them. I wondered if their mother had done away with them. "Where are they?" I demanded when she showed up for her evening meal. The tired cat looked at me a second then quietly ate her food. I decided the babies were really gone and became very angry. "Okay, kitty-cat, no babies, no special treatment!" I told her, and gave her less food the next day.

But that old guilt hit me again. What if she were still feeding them somewhere? And aside from that, she was becoming so emaciated it was painful to look at her. She reminded me of Norman, who was steadily losing weight and looking so fragile he could break in half.

A week later she was in the barn waiting for me to fill her dish when something caught my eye. It was a little black head peering at me from a crack between two bales of hay. I froze and waited. A little gray head appeared too. I looked at their weary mother and shamefully conceded, "I guess I had no faith in you. I hope you'll accept my apology." I said nearly the same thing to Norman when I finally learned his sister had been stricken with Alzheimer's disease the year before, and he had been exhausting himself caring for her.

Each day I watched the gray cat pull her kittens toward her

to feed them. I don't know how she did it. She became thinner and thinner, and I prayed for the day her babies would be weaned so she could rest.

Then, one day, the kittens began eating food from their mother's bowl, and the next morning the gray cat wasn't waiting at the hydrant for me. When she finally showed up she was breathing strangely and wouldn't eat. She just rested a while in the sun and then disappeared. It worried me more when she didn't show up for her evening meal. I put a bowl of food in the barn for the kittens and kept them company while they ate.

While I watched the kittens, the gray cat appeared. She rubbed against my leg as she walked slowly past me. Her eyes a bit out of focus and breathing with great difficulty, she lay down and seemed to wait. I petted her while the kittens lay next to her. Then I left them alone together.

The next morning I took a shirt from my closet and carried a shovel down to the barn, where I found what I knew I would find. I wrapped the gray cat in my shirt and buried her next to the stream winding through my property. Then I prayed the Twenty-third Psalm and, as though she could still hear me, whispered, "I loved you, gray cat."

Right then it struck me hard that I had never given her a name. I ran back to the barn and picked up her two babies. "Your name is Tiger," I told the striped kitten. "And your name is Hoppy," I said to the black one, who had a funny little walk.

As they scampered away, I thought about the gray cat, who, like Norman, I had condemned before knowing the facts. I closed my eyes and promised God I would try breaking my awful habit of jumping to conclusions. Then I thanked him for Norman, and for the kittens who now greet me down at the hydrant the way their mother had.

Precious

MARY JANE STRETCH

I drive very slowly when I turn into my driveway after dark, because it's not unusual to see a herd of deer ahead of me. I always turn off my lights, roll down my window, and talk to them softly as I inch past them. Although I can't tell one from another, I'm sure that some of them came to The Aark as fawns and were released when they were old enough to take care of themselves. I often wonder if, in some way, they remember me. . . .

In the spring, in May, when does are giving birth, people bring us fawns. Most of them are found along Swamp Road, a busy two-lane road with high embankments and fields on each side. Usually the fawns are only a day or two old, and my guess is that they were born in the fields close to the embankment and then tumbled down onto the road because they weren't steady on their feet yet. Sometimes people find them in a field where the mother may have left them while she went to graze. Normally the baby will stay there, absolutely still, until the mother comes back to nurse it. Staying still is a fawn's only defense against predators, and at that early age it doesn't have a scent. But people can walk right up to a fawn and pick it up, which they do all too often. They mean well, but they don't know how to look for signs of the mother before they move the fawn. If they don't see her, they assume she isn't there.

Whenever possible, we try to put a fawn back where the mother can find it. Of course, if the mother was seen dead on the road, or if the fawn was found by the body of a dead doe, then the fawn should be sheltered. And if we can't tell which field is the right one, then we don't try putting it back. But if the fawn was found in a field, and if we can find the right one, then the chances are good that its mother will come back for it. . . .

I believe that loving wild things means letting them go. We don't have the right to hold onto them.

I learned that lesson back in 1976 from a doe that was brought to me when she was a day old. She was my first fawn, and it was my first year as a full-time rehabber. A game warden found her on a road, and when he handed her to me he said, "Call her Precious—she's so precious!" I couldn't resist her or the name. I knew a lot about deer, but I had never raised a fawn, so she was not only adorable but fascinating. I carried her under my arm with one hand under her chest so that her legs could dangle free. Fawn legs should never be restricted because they're very fragile. If you hold their legs tightly when they want to kick out, they'll kick out anyway and might break a leg. . . .

I hadn't intended to call her anything, except perhaps "Little One," a name I use for many animals. But since she was my first fawn, I fussed over her and did some things I wouldn't do now. Besides, I don't know anyone who can keep her hands off a fawn. From the beginning Precious was friendly and affectionate. She let me hold her face to help her drink from her bottle, and not all fawns will do that. Her fur at that young age was longer and softer than the fur of a full-grown doe because it was meant to keep her warm. It was fuzzy, too, and wherever she licked herself she left unruly little cowlicks that I simply had to touch. She was all ears and eyes when she looked at me, and if I put my head close to hers, I got kissed. Fawns like to lick the salt off your skin, so if you're within range, that's what happens. I can assure you, when you're depressed there's nothing in the whole universe better than fawn kisses to make you feel better. Nothing! If I could bottle them, I'd be a millionaire.

Today, when fawns come in, we put them in a playpen or let them loose in the office for a few days. If they're in a playpen, they learn how to jump out very quickly. They're not steady on their legs yet, and they slip on the vinyl tile, so we put mover's quilts on the floor. We didn't use playpens when we had Precious; instead, we kept her in the kitchen for about five days until she learned to identify us as a source of food. She made herself comfortable in a corner out of the way, and when the girls and I called her, she would come to us, still teetery on her long slender legs, eager for her bottle. Fawns drink a lot of milk. For the first five days we have them, while they're in the nursery, we give them as many as five bottles a day, and these bottles hold two quarts. In the wild, the deer mothers don't feed their fawns frequently and usually let them tank up when they do, so we let them nurse the same way. Once we let the fawns go free, we feed them on demand, which is usually about two or three bottles a day. Very quickly they get down to one bottle, and then none.

After a few days, Precious began to follow us outside. We let her come along, but the girls and I took turns walking with her so she wouldn't wander off and get lost. She was still tiny and there were foxes in the area. Our inexperience made us overprotective of her because we didn't know what to expect. But she got away from us anyway. We'd see her one minute and she'd be gone the next. She was so beautifully camouflaged that we would walk right past her without seeing her. Then suddenly she'd show up again.

Finally I began to realize that she was the teacher and we were the students. "We're going to do things her way," I told the girls. "We'll put her out in the morning, and we *won't* stay with her." Of course, I worried about her. I had handled her so much that I was bonded to her. She was becoming like one of my dogs, a member of the family. I kept reminding myself that she wasn't domesticated and would have to be released, but my heart wasn't listening to what my head was saying. After I put her out each morning, I was uneasy until she came back for food. I always fed her at the same door, and she'd come in and stand there, hollering and kicking the door, when she was hungry for her bottle. Deer make a bleating sound, like sheep, but sometimes louder, and I was always relieved when I heard her. By the time she was a month old she had dropped down to two bottles a day, and she'd wander off again as soon as she finished them. . . .

At night we made more of an effort to find her and bring her into the house because I was afraid of foxes. But I made a mistake in doing that because I conditioned her to come inside at night and that isn't the natural way of deer. They're nocturnal animals. And eventually Precious let me know that she wasn't like a dog or a cat. She wanted to be free.

For a while she was half pet, half wild thing. She loved to play with the children and she'd let them dress her up like a doll. She got along very well with my dogs, but when another dog came onto the property she disappeared. Fortunately she knew the difference. But she began to resist us a little more as time went on. She was away longer, sometimes for more than a day. She was growing up and was too big for us to pick up and put down, so she was able to go her own way. She was off her bottle but she came in for treats. I used to carry granola cookies in my pocket just in case she showed up. Sometimes she'd follow the kids into the house after playing with them, and I'd find her asleep on the sofa. . . .

Precious was a lovely young doe with sleek taupe fur when the hunting season arrived, and even though we used to patrol our land on horseback, poachers still got in. I was sick at the thought that Precious might be shot. I tried to keep her close to home until February, when the season was over. At night I would coax her into the barn with treats. To protect her in daylight I spray-painted a big ABSOLUTELY NO on her sides, but she licked it off. So we tied ribbons around her neck to notify hunters that she was a hand-raised animal and to warn them off shooting her. There was a danger in the ribbons, too, because if they got caught on something she could have hurt herself trying to pull free. But we had to weigh that against the risk of her getting shot. The ribbons got frayed and some fell off, but we kept adding more until there were so many around her neck that only a truly horrible person would have taken aim at and shot her.

I have wonderful memories of Precious playing with my children that winter. She loved the snow as much as they did, and it was so much fun for her to chase them up and down the hills when they went sledding. She was much more sure-footed than they were in their boots and leggings, and she would leap over them and their sleds, always getting to the bottom of the hill before they did. If they fell off their sleds, she'd go back and lick them and start jumping over them again. She infuriated them with her agility.

"She's a pain in the neck!" Sammy complained. "We can't even sled with her around."

"She's rough, Mom!" Debbie summed it up. "She's not little

anymore." Sometimes I'd take Precious into the house for a while so the girls could sled without interruption. They were so accustomed to living among wild animals that they wouldn't appreciate what a rare experience it was for anyone to go sledding with a deer. Perhaps someday they would treasure the memory. . . .

As spring came we saw less of her, and she shared fewer of our daytime hours. She was becoming more nocturnal, which was perfectly right and natural. But I worried about her. If she didn't come in for two or three days, I was sure she'd been hit by a car, and we'd go driving around to see if there were any dead deer in the road. I was also afraid she might have dragged herself into a field and died after being hit. Then she'd show up, eat a cookie, and vanish again. Releasing her was so hard. I didn't know how the system was supposed to work, because I didn't have a system. Precious was giving it to me a little at a time, but I didn't understand the rules yet or know what the next step was. There were many anxious moments, many heart-stopping days.

Finally I had to let go: it was the only thing I could do. I had done all I could to protect her. I couldn't do any more. When she stayed away for several days at a time, I began to get used to it. I didn't even look for her. I assumed she was all right.

We knew she had joined a herd of deer. We used to see them in the fields almost every day, and sometimes Precious would break out of the herd and come to us. Once she was grown, we couldn't distinguish her from other does except by her behavior—deer don't normally leave a herd and walk up to people. We knew it was Precious, and all we had to do was call her by name and she'd come closer. The rest of the herd stayed apart. They'd wait and stamp their feet and snort until she went back to them, but none of them ever came to us.

One morning in late spring, I was out in a field behind the house when I saw a doe and two fawns coming toward me. I stood very still so I wouldn't alarm them. The fawns were about two weeks old, old enough to follow their mother. Then the doe did something very unusual. She saw me, yet she brought her fawns halfway across the field and let them graze just a little distance from where I stood. It had to be Precious! A wild doe doesn't bring babies that close to a human being.

"Oh, Precious! Oh, Precious!" I said. "Oh, they're beautiful! Oh, Precious!" I was so touched by the loveliness of what I saw that I cried.

I didn't move toward them and they didn't come any closer, but they stayed long enough for me to look at them carefully. I had no doubt that it was Precious come to show me her babies—two tiny, delicate, cream-spotted, honey-colored fawns, all eyes, ears, and legs. Then she took them away and didn't come back. She had become wild enough to sense that human beings are a threat, yet she remembered enough of her association with me to let me know she was doing well in her natural environment. It was the biggest thank you she could possibly give me. In spite of all the mistakes I had made, because she was my first fawn and I had so much to learn, she was telling me that she had survived, reproduced, and was all right. I hoped she would live for several more years.

from THE SWAN IN MY BATHTUB

Maxie

ANONYMOUS

I remember the first time I saw you at a farm in North Carolina, one little black-and-white face in a group of nine. You saw me, you walked over to me, you picked me. That was the beginning of a ten-year friendship like none I have ever known or experienced.

Our relationship started in Goldsboro, North Carolina, and ended up here in Seattle. As we made our journey from North Carolina to Minnesota to California to Arizona, and then to Washington, the only thing we needed was each other, that along with a job from time to time to keep us warm and our stomachs full. I remember a painful time in my life when I had to leave you with my parents for two years. I never stopped thinking about you and took comfort in knowing you were loved and cared for. I'll also never forget how you knew me the moment you saw me when I came back to get you, and from that moment on, I swore we were never to be parted again.

You gave meaning to each and every day that you were with me, comforted me when I was sad, inspired me when I was confused, loved me when I felt I had no love. I never again thought about not having you with me forever, but I feel I never took the time we did have together for granted. I thank

God that you found me, and I have been made richer by the experience.

I knew it was time to finally let you go when you were suffering from brain tumors. The idea of letting you go pained me more than anything I had ever felt before. I was racked with guilt and pain, and I'm sorry I couldn't hide that from you. But I also know that you understood; and that night, as you looked at me in my eyes, you also knew what was happening. I let you go, Maxie, because I loved you, but my memory of you is something I will cling to till the day I die. You continue to comfort me; and though I long to hold you again, I can close my eyes and feel you and know that you are near.

from OUR BEST FRIENDS

ACKNOWLEDGMENTS

(continued from page ii)

"Do You Remember Me?" is from *The Rufus Chronicle* by C. W. Gusewelle. Copyright 1996 C. W. Gusewelle. Published by The Ballantine Publishing Group.

"Loyalty Is Serious Business" is from *Stillmeadow Sampler* by Gladys Taber. © 1959 Gladys Taber.

"We Called Him Romeo" is from *Sasha's Tail* by Jacqueline Damian. © 1995 Jacqueline Damian. Published by W. W. Norton & Company.

"Rupa and I—a Reason to Live," by Maureen Keenan-Mason, and "Help Me, Keesha!" and "Night Visitor," by Jackie Geyer, are from *Animals As Teachers & Healers* by Susan Chernak McElroy. © 1996, 1997 Susan Chernak McElroy. Published by The Ballantine Publishing Group.

"The Mouser-Cat" by Anna Moretti is from *Cat Caught My Heart* by Michael Capuzzo and Teresa Banik Capuzzo. © 1998 Michael Capuzzo and Teresa Banik Capuzzo. Published by Bantam Books.

"No More Ghosts" is from *A Search for the Perfect Dog* by Gary Shiebler. © 1997 Gary Shiebler. Published by Broadway Books.

"Earthquake!" is from *The Compassion of Animals* by Kristin von Kreisler. © 1997 Kristin von Kreisler. Published by Prima Publishing.

"Remembering Rufus" is from *The Rufus Chronicle* by C. W. Gusewelle. Copyright 1996 C. W. Gusewelle. Published by The Ballantine Publishing Group.

"Priorities" by Terri Crisp is from *Chicken Soup for the Pet Lover's Soul* by Jack Canfield, Mark Victor Hansen, Marty Becker, D.V.M., Carol Kline. © 1998 Jack Canfield, Mark Victor Hansen, Marty Backer and Carol Kline. Published by Health Communications, Inc.

"As Close As My Shadow" is from *Stillmeadow Sampler* by Gladys Taber. © 1959 Gladys Taber.

"Leaving the Fast Lane" by Larry Chamberlain is from *Animals As Teachers & Healers* by Susan Chernak McElroy. © 1996, 1997 Susan Chernak McElroy. Published by The Ballantine Publishing Group.

"Loving Jasper" is from *Living With Dogs* by Henry and Mary Ellen Korman. © 1997 by Henry Korman and Mary Ellen Korman. Published by Wildcat Canyon Press.

"The Best Part of Our Day" is from *Getting My Goat* by M. J. Arrison. Copyright 1996 by Margret J. Arrison. Used by permission of the author.

"Green Eggs and Sam" by Penny Porter is from *The Reader's Digest,* May 1999.

"A Lived-In House" is from *Stillmeadow Sampler* by Gladys Taber. © 1959 Gladys Taber.

"Till We Meet Again" is from *The Best Cat Ever* by Cleveland Amory. © 1993 Cleveland Amory. Published by Little, Brown and Company.

"The Dog Who Found Me" is from *Dogs Never Lie About Love* by Jeffrey Moussaieff Masson. © 1997 Jeffrey Masson. Published by Crown Publishers, Inc.

"Ginny's First Cat" is from *The Dog Who Rescues Cats* by Philip Gonzalez and Leonore Fleischer. © 1995 Philip Gonzalez. Published by HarperCollins Publishers.

"Rocky" by Terri L. Collins is from *Our Best Friends* by Michael Capuzzo and Teresa Banik Capuzzo. © 1998 Michael Capuzzo and Teresa Banik Capuzzo. Published by Bantam Books.

"To Eloise With Love" is from *It's a Jungle Out There* by Gary Richmond. © 1996 Harvest House Publishers.

"Precious" is from *The Swan in My Bathtub* by Mary Jane Stretch. © 1991 Mary Jane Stretch. Published by The Penguin Group.

"Maxie" is from *Our Best Friends* by Michael Capuzzo and Teresa Banik Capuzzo. © 1998 Michael Capuzzo and Teresa Banik Capuzzo. Published by Bantam Books.

A Note from the Editors

This original Guideposts series was created by the Book and Inspirational Media Division of the company that publishes *Guideposts,* a monthly magazine filled with true stories of people's adventures in faith. *Guideposts* is not sold on the newsstand. It's available by subscription only. And subscribing is easy. All you have to do is write to Guideposts, 39 Seminary Hill Road, Carmel, New York 10512. When you subscribe, each month you can count on receiving exciting new evidence of God's presence, His guidance and His limitless love for all of us.

Guideposts is also available on the Internet by accessing our home page on the World Wide Web at www.guideposts.org. Send prayer requests to our Monday morning Prayer Fellowship. Read stories from recent issues of our magazines, *Guideposts, Angels on Earth, Guideposts for Kids* and *Positive Living,* and follow our popular book of daily devotionals, *Daily Guideposts.* Excerpts from some of our best-selling books are also available.